THE CHILD'S RAINY DAY BOOK

LECTOR HOUSE PUBLIC DOMAIN WORKS

HAPPY READING!

THE CHILD'S RAINY DAY BOOK

MARY WHITE

ISBN: 978-93-5614-223-7

Published: 1905

© 2022
LECTOR HOUSE LLP

LECTOR HOUSE

LECTOR HOUSE LLP
E-MAIL: lectorpublishing@gmail.com

Building a Piece of Pottery with Coils of Clay—as the Indians do

THE CHILD'S RAINY DAY BOOK

BY

MARY WHITE

ILLUSTRATED BY
THE AUTHOR

1905

Published, October, 1905

TO MY SISTER
ANNA WHITE SHERMAN
AND HER CHILDREN
ROGER, HERBERT, ELIZABETH, ROSAMOND AND ANNA

CONTENTS

LIST OF ILLUSTRATIONS

LIST OF FIGURES

CHILD'S RAINY DAY BOOK

CHAPTER I

A FOREWORD TO MOTHERS

How shall we answer the ever recurring rainy day question, "What shall I do?" We hear it wherever children are kept indoors—from whatever cause. All of us are concerned with the answer—mothers, fathers, teachers, big brothers and sisters—even maiden aunts. We all know what is coming when Jack turns from the rain-splashed window with a listless face and Dorothy, none too gently, thrusts her favourite doll into the corner with its face to the wall.

One might suppose that, with the hosts of mechanical toys, of costly French dolls, each with a wardrobe as much in keeping with fashion as that of a society woman, the small sons and daughters would be content for a year of rainy days. But that proves how little one knows about it. Such toys are too perfect, too complete, and very soon they are pushed into the background.

The boy's real treasures are the willow whistle that Uncle Tom taught him to make last summer, the boat that he is building and the game he invented—a favourite one with all the children. Bedtime and getting-up time for the French doll may come and go, while she lies forgotten in the corner, for is there not a dress to be made for the clothespin doll?

We need only to look back about twenty years to realise how natural all this is. What do we remember? Not the toys that were brought us when father and mother went on a journey. They are very hazy—these visions of a doll in silk and lace, and a donkey with real hair and a nodding head. What became of them afterward? We forget. But the games we "made up," the paper dolls we cut from fashion papers, the target we laboured to make of coiled straw—these are as fresh in our memories as if we had played with them yesterday.

Shall we not answer the question by giving the children something to do, not by entertaining them but by helping them to entertain themselves.

CHAPTER II
SIMPLE HOME-MADE TOYS AND GAMES

A Bean Bag Game

Materials Required: ½ yard each of blue, red, yellow and green gingham,

3 quarts of small white beans,

A length of No. 6 rattan,

A bunch of red raffia,

A tapestry needle,

3 screw eyes,

2 ½ yards of strong twine,

A spool of No. 40 white cotton,

A needle,

Scissors.

Very many good games can be played with bean bags. The following is a simple one to prepare.

Cut from blue gingham three pieces, each five inches wide by twelve long. Other pieces of the same size are cut from red, yellow and green gingham—three of each colour. These pieces are made up into bags by doubling them and stitching up the sides with strong thread; leaving one end of each open. This will give a small girl something to do for more than one rainy day.

When they have all been stitched, fill each bag half full of small, white beans, turn in the edges of the open end and sew it up, over and over, with strong thread. Be very careful to sew the seams securely, for if you do you will have a good, durable bag instead of one from which the beans are always dropping.

The other part of the game is a large ring of rattan ten inches across, which is made as follows:

Soak a piece of No. 6 rattan in water for a few minutes. While you are waiting for it to get pliable thread a tapestry or darning needle with red raffia. Whittle an end of the rattan into a long point. Next coil the rattan into a ring, ten inches across; lay the end of your raffia, with its tip turned to the right, on the rattan ring and bring the needle, threaded with raffia, around and over the ring. The raffia is then brought under the long end of rattan, around it and down under the ring, binding the second coil of rattan to the first with what is called a "Figure Eight" stitch (see Fig. 1). Hold the ring firmly in your left hand while you sew with the right. First under and around the lower coil, then up, under and around the upper one. It is pretty work, besides making such a firm, light ring.

Playing the Bean Bag Game

When you have bound the second coil to the first almost all the way round the ring, cut the rattan so that it will overlap the beginning of the ring about an inch, and whittle it to a long, flat point. Continue the Figure Eight stitch as far as you can, then bind the raffia round and round the ring, and sew back and forth through the raffia covering till it is secure. You can then cut it close to the ring.

Fig. 1

Fasten a screw eye at the top of the frame of the playroom door and one on each side of the doorway, on the edge of the frame, four feet and a half from the floor.

Rattan Ring

Tie a piece of strong twine, about a yard long, at the top of the ring and another, three-quarters of a yard, on each side. Fasten the upper string to the screw eye above the doorway so that the ring will hang with its lower edge about four feet from the floor. Tie the other strings through the screw eyes to right and left of the doorway. The game is now complete. From two to four children can play it. Each has three bean bags of one colour and takes his turn at throwing them through the ring, standing on a mark eight feet from the doorway. One player keeps the score, and whenever a bean bag is sent through the ring the child who threw it is credited with five points. The one who first succeeds in making fifty points is the winner.

A Book House for Paper Dolls

Materials Required: A large blank book with a stiff cover, and preferably with unruled pages,

A number of old magazines,

Some pieces of wall paper the size of the book's pages,

Several pieces of lace or other fancy paper,

A tube of paste,

Scissors.

Any little girl who is looking for a home for a family of paper dolls will find a book the very best kind of a house for them. And then such fun as it will be to furnish it! First comes the house hunting. A large new blank book with unruled pages would be best of all, and that is what we want if we can get it, but of course all doll families cannot live in such luxury. An old account book with most of its pages unused will make an excellent house. I have even known a family of dolls to be cheerful and happy in an old city directory.

It will be easy to find furniture in the advertising pages of magazines, rugs can be cut from pictures in the same magazines and bits of wall paper are used for the walls of the book house. Tissue paper of different colours and papers with a lace edge make charming window curtains, while thicker fancy papers may be used for portieres. On the cover of the book a picture of the house, or just the doorway, may be pasted. The first two pages are of course the hall. For this you will need a broad staircase, hall seat, hardwood floor and rugs, with perhaps an open fireplace or a cushioned window seat to make it look hospitable. Try to find furniture all about the same size, or if you cannot do this put the smaller pieces at the back of the room and the larger ones toward the front.

Next there will be the drawing room to furnish, then the library, the dining room and pantry, not forgetting the kitchen and laundry. Use two pages for each room, leaving several between the different rooms, so that the book shall not be too full at the front and empty at the back. If it does not close easily remove some of the blank pages. Cut out the different pieces of furniture as carefully as possible, paste them in as neatly as you can, and you will have a book house to be proud of.

Flowered papers will be the best for the bedrooms, or plain wall papers in light colours; and with brass bedsteads, pretty little dressing tables and curtains made of thin white tissue paper (which looks so like white muslin), they will be as dainty as can be. Now and then through the book it is interesting to have a page with just a bay window and a broad window seat with cushions and pillows—as if it were a part of a long hall. Hang curtains of coloured or figured paper in front of it so that they will have to be lifted if anyone wants to peep in. When you have finished the bathroom, playroom, maids' rooms and attic there will still be the piazza, the garden, the stables and the golf course (covering several pages), to arrange. If you have a paint box and can colour tastefully you will be able to make your book house even more attractive than it is already.

Planning a Book House

United States Mail

Materials Required: A pasteboard box, about 3 by 6 inches,

Some old white pasteboard boxes with a glossy finish,

A box of paints,

3 unused postal cards,

A tube of paste,

Pen and ink,

Scissors.

Fig. 2

This is a fine game for rainy days. Any boy can make it and if he likes to use pencil and paint brush he will find it as interesting to make as to play with. Get a small pasteboard box about six inches long by three wide and an inch deep—such as spools of cotton come in. Cover it with white paper, pasting it neatly and securely. Then draw and colour on the lid a mail bag, which should almost cover it—either a brown leather sack or a white canvas one with "United States Mail" on it in large blue letters. Do not forget to draw the holes at the top of the bag and the rope which passes through them to close it. You have now something to hold the counters for the game. These are made to look like letters and postal cards. To make the letters, rule a set of lines three-quarters of an inch apart, across a box or cover of shiny white cardboard. Then another set, crossing the others at right angles. These should be an inch and a quarter apart. The postal cards are ruled in the same way (on real, unused postal cards), so as to make oblong spaces. Cut these out with a sharp pair of scissors. There should be thirty cardboard pieces and at least twenty-five of the postal cards. Now draw on the cards, with a fine pen and black ink, marks like those on a postal card—the stamp in the corner, the lettering and the address. Make pen lines on all of the pasteboard letters like Fig. 2 and paint a tiny red dot on each to look like sealing-wax. On the reverse side of one write something to look like an address, and paint in large letters "D.L.O.," (to stand for Dead Letter Office) in the corner. Six other letters are also addressed in the same way, but have instead of "D.L.O." a red stamp and a blue one, the latter wider than it is high, to represent a Special Delivery stamp. Nine pieces should also be cut from brown cardboard in the shape shown in Fig. 3 to represent pack-ages. Paint three red stamps in the corner of each of these.

Rules for Playing United States Mail

Fig. 3

Two or more persons can play this game. When the pieces are equally divided among the players, the one on the right of the dealer throws a piece on the table, saying as he does so, "I send a letter to B— —," for example, and then counts five, not running the numbers in together, but as deliberately as a clock ticks. Before he has stopped counting, the player on his right must name a city or town beginning with B. If he succeeds in doing this he wins the piece, otherwise it goes to the player who threw it. When all the pieces have been played each player counts his score.

The value of the pieces is as follows: Each postal card counts one, each letter two, each package six. The Special Delivery letters are worth ten points each, and the person who is so unfortunate as to have the letter with "D.L.O." upon it loses ten points from his score.

Flying Rings

Materials Required: A flour-barrel top,

¾ yard of yellow cheesecloth,

5 large wire nails,

3 lengths of No. 4 rattan,

A bunch of red raffia,

A bunch of green raffia,

A bunch of yellow raffia,

A tapestry needle,

Some small tacks,

A hammer,

A tube of glue,

A sheet of note paper.

Boys and girls will enjoy this game, and both can help in making it. The materials are simple and easily obtained, which is also an advantage. First of all we shall need a flour-barrel top. This should be covered with yellow cheesecloth drawn smooth and tight and tacked in place along the outer edge. Measure with a rule to find the exact centre and make a pencil mark on the cheesecloth at that point. Another mark is made above this one, half way between it and the edge. A third mark is placed at the right of the middle one and half way between it and the edge, as well as one to the left and one below it at the same distance from the centre. A large nail is driven into the barrel top at each of the five marks (see Fig. 4). Two screw eyes are then put in at the top, about a foot apart, so that it can be easily hung. Next draw on note paper that is not too stiff the figures 5, 10, 15, 25 and 50. Make them about an inch high and quite thick and go over them with ink. With a small pair of scissors cut out these numbers and paste each under a nail, as shown in Fig. 4.

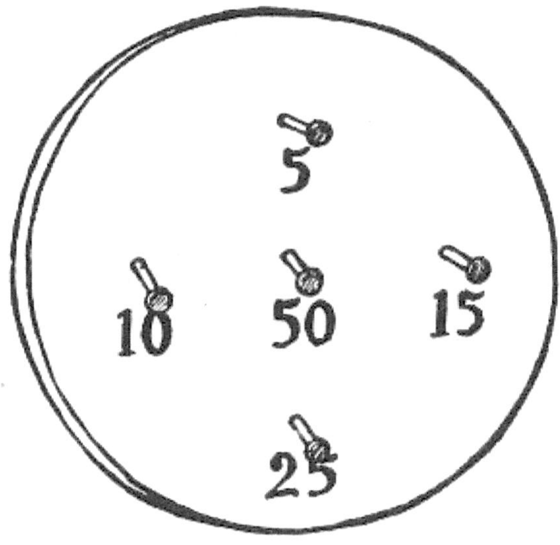

Fig. 4

Next there are the rings to be made. Follow the directions given on pages 6 and 7, using No. 4 rattan instead of No. 6, and these rings should only be two and a half inches across. Make three rings of each colour, green, red and yellow, and the game is complete.

To Play It:

Hang the barrel top on the wall or against a screen and see who can throw the most rings on the nails standing six feet away. Each player has three rings of a different colour, and each in turn throws his rings at the mark. When he succeeds in tossing a ring on one of the nails he scores as many points as the number under the nail indicates.

How to Make a Cork Castle

Materials Required: A number of old corks, the larger the better,

A tube of glue,

A penknife,

A piece of pasteboard a foot square,

A sheet of dull green tissue paper.

Such fascinating castles can be made from old corks—or if you live near a cork factory you can get plenty of odds and ends of cork bark that will be even better for the purpose. With a penknife cut small bricks, half an inch long by quarter of an inch wide and an eighth of an inch thick. If you are planning a round tower, such as is shown in Fig. 5, make the bricks in the wedge shape shown in Fig. 6. Cut them as nearly alike as possible, but it will do no harm if they are not perfectly regular; the castle will only look more ancient and interesting. It is wonderful how much the bits of cork look like stone.

Fig. 5

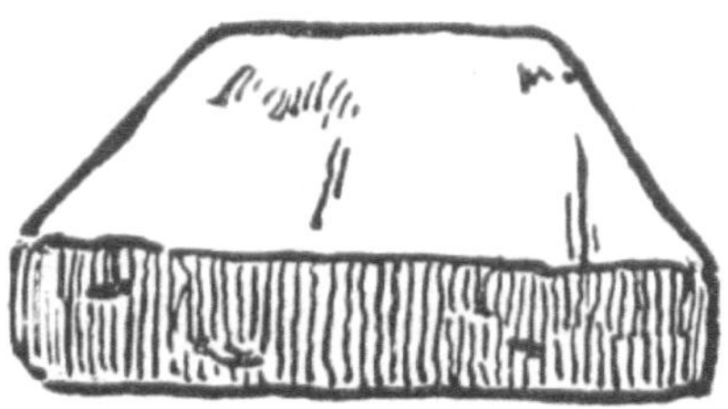

Fig. 6

When you have a good supply of bricks ready you may begin to build. Use glue to stick the blocks together; the kind that comes in a tube is the easiest and cleanest to handle. Leave spaces for doors and windows, and for the roof use a large flat cork from a preserve jar. Mark it off into battlements such as are shown in Fig. 5, and cut them out carefully. Then glue the roof securely on the walls of the castle.

Where shall we place it now that it is made? A green mountain side is a good location for a castle, and it can be made quite easily. Bend a piece of pasteboard about a foot square (an old box cover will do) into dents that will almost break it, these look quite like hills and valleys and sharp crags, especially when they have been covered with green tissue paper. To do this spread a layer of paste or glue all over the pasteboard and then press the paper upon it. If it wrinkles, so much the better, for it will look more like grass and growing things.

A Doll's Shaker Bonnet

Materials Required: A piece of fine straw about 4 x 6 inches,

Some scraps of plain-coloured china silk,

½ yard of straw-coloured ribbon, ¼ of an inch wide,

½ yard of narrow ribbon the colour of the china silk,

A spool of straw-coloured sewing silk.

Fig. 7

The daintiest little Shaker bonnet may be easily made by a little girl to fit one of her dolls. From the brim of an old leghorn, or other fine straw hat, cut two pieces, the shapes shown in Figs. 7 and 8. For a doll six or eight inches long the front piece will need to be about five inches long by an inch and a half wide. Bind the curved edge of the front piece with the straw-coloured ribbon, sewing it through and through with small stitches, using straw-coloured sewing silk. Sew one edge of a piece of the straw-coloured ribbon close to the curved edge of the back piece from A to AA (see Fig. 8). Mark, with a pencil, a dot at the middle of the curved edge of the back portion and one at the middle of the straight edge of the front part. Pin the two parts together at these dots and sew the edges together. In doing this you will have to turn back the ribbon which edges the back portion. Next bring the ribbon forward to cover the rough edges of the straw where the two parts join and sew its loose edge along on the front portion. Cut a piece of China silk seven and three-quarters inches long by an inch and three-quarters wide. Make a narrow hem all around it. A tiny pencil mark is then made on the lower edge of the back piece and another at the middle of the silk strip. Gather the silk just below the hem on the upper edge and sew it to the lower edge of the bonnet at the back. Stitch a piece of narrow ribbon eight inches long at each side of the front, for strings, and the bonnet is done.

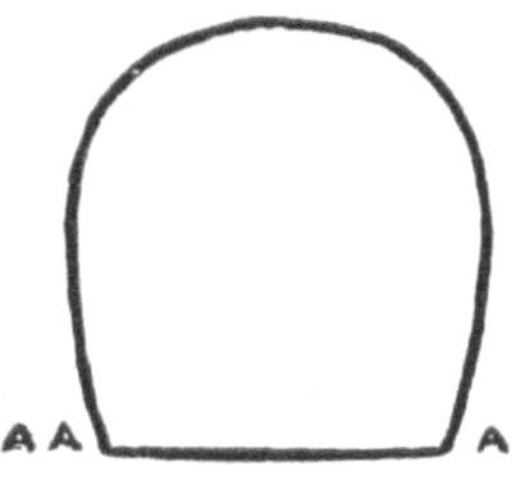

Fig. 8

Leather and String Puzzle

Materials Required: A strip of thick leather, 7 inches long by 2 wide,
A piece of heavy linen string a foot long,
A knife.

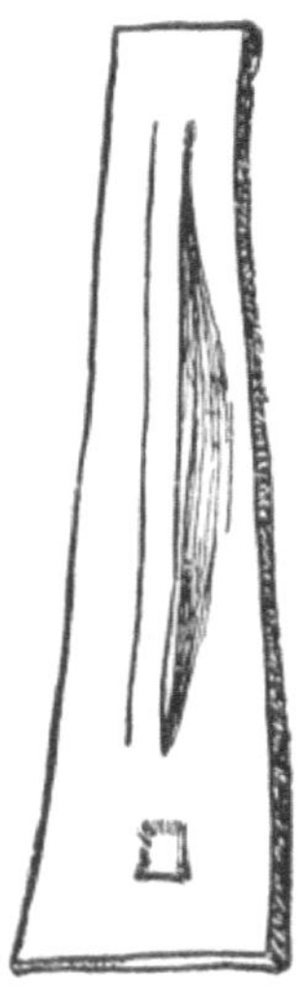

Fig. 9

With a sharp knife, a small strip of leather and a bit of strong string any boy can make this simple puzzle. It is easier to make, however, than it is to do, as the boy's friends will discover. Fig. 9 will show how it is made. A strip of leather five and a half inches long, an inch and a quarter wide at one end and five-eighths of an inch at the other, is first cut. Then, starting at about five-eighths of an inch from the narrow end, cut with a sharp knife two slits down the middle of the piece three-eighths of an inch apart and three inches long. At three-eighths of an inch from the wide end a small piece, one-quarter of an inch square, is cut out of the middle of the strip (see Fig. 9). From the scraps of leather remaining cut two pieces, each one inch long by five-eighths of an inch wide. Make a hole in the middle of each. Then pass a piece of stout linen cord eleven inches long back of the long, open strip in the large piece of leather, leaving the ends of equal length. Pass both ends down through the square hole and tie each of them securely through the hole in the middle of one of the small pieces of leather. This completes it.

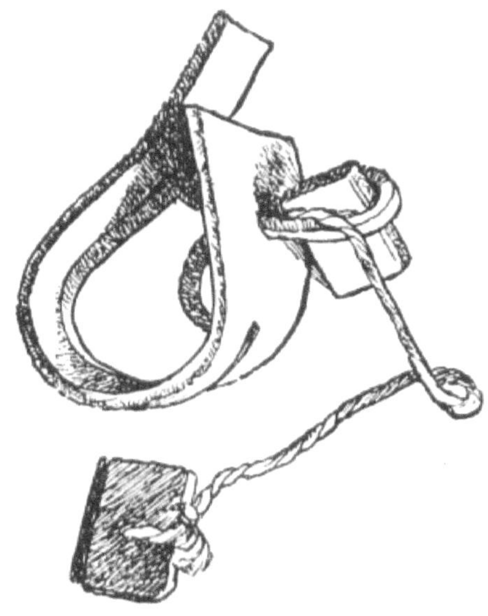

Fig. 10

The object is to try to get the string, with the small piece of leather at either end, off the large piece of leather without cutting or untying it. The only way to do this is shown in Fig. 10. Holding both ends of the string, close to where it passes back of the narrow strip in the middle of the large piece of leather, pull the strip out through the small square hole. One of the small pieces of leather can then be slipped through the loop thus formed, releasing the string.

A Bed for a Little Doll

Materials Required: An oblong pasteboard box an inch or more longer than the doll it is to hold,

½ yard of flowered or striped muslin,

¼ yard of blue and white seersucker or other cotton,

Some cotton or wool wadding,

½ yard of thin white cotton cloth,

¼ yard of outing flannel,

¼ yard of white piqué.

Almost any little girl who chooses to do so can make this dainty bed for one of her small dolls. She will only need an oblong pasteboard box with a cover, and large enough to hold the doll comfortably. If mamma will let her have some pieces of cotton, flowered, striped and plain and a little cotton or wool wadding, she will have all the materials she needs.

First cut from blue and white striped cotton a bag the length and width of the box. Stitch it neatly together around three sides, turn it right side out and fill it with cotton or wool wadding. Turn in the edges on the fourth side and sew them together over and over. With a darning needle threaded with blue cotton or silk the mattress can be tufted here and there. The needle is first run through to the under side, then one little stitch is taken, bringing the thread back again to the right side, where the two ends are tied tightly together and cut close to the knot. If these tufts are made at equal distances, say one inch apart, all over the mattress it will make it look very "real."

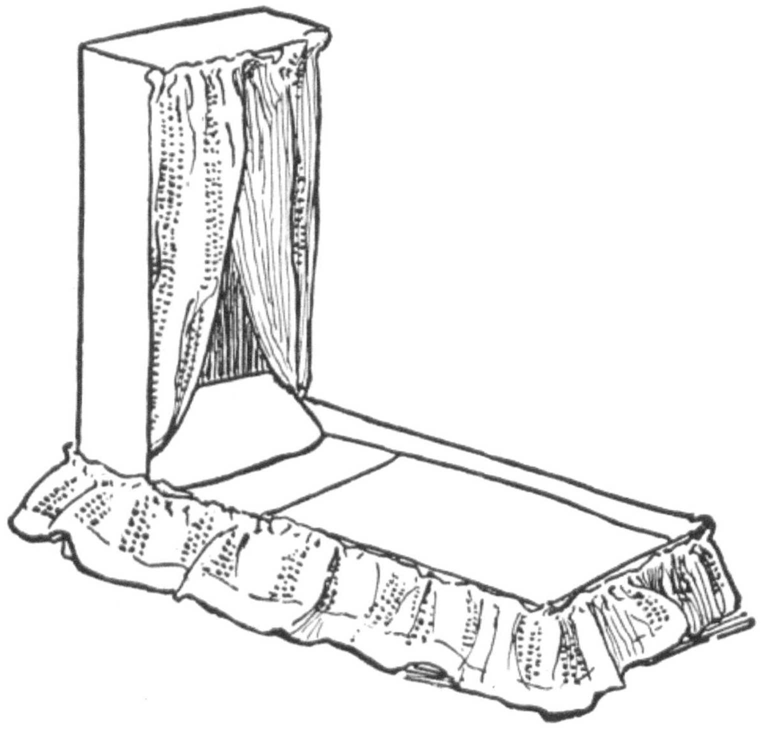

Fig. 11

The pillow is made in the same way as the mattress, except that it is not tufted. Cut the sheets and pillowcase from thin white cotton, allowing enough for hems. Make the pillowcase a quarter of an inch wider and about an inch and a quarter longer than the pillow. Stitch it around both sides and on one end and hem the other end. Tiny blankets may be cut from outing flannel, and a spread made from a piece of white piqué or other thick white wash material. The bed can now be made up, but it will look very plain. A fluffy canopy and valance (or flounce) of flowered or striped white muslin will improve it wonderfully. The cover is set on end and the head of the bedstead is pressed into it (see Fig. 11), making a frame for the canopy. Measure from the front corner of this frame to the middle of the front and cut a piece of muslin half again as wide as this measurement and long enough to reach from the top of the frame to the bottom of the bed. Another piece the same size is cut, and then both are turned in and gathered at the top, hemmed on the other edges and sewed into place on the top edge of the canopy frame, so that the two will meet in the middle. They are both looped back against the front edge of the frame, see Fig. 11, and sewed there securely. The valance or flounce around the lower part of the bed is cut wide enough to allow for hemming at the bottom and to turn in at the top. It should be long enough to reach once and a half around the bed. Turn in the upper edge of the valance, gather it to fit the bed and pin it in position. Then sew it with a strong needle and coarse thread on to the box through and through. This makes as comfortable and pretty a bed as dolly could wish.

Floor Baseball

Materials Required: A piece of white chalk,

A piece of sheet lead, 2 by 2 inches, and as thick as a fifty-cent piece,

3 or 4 strands of scarlet raffia,

A tapestry needle,

A gimlet.

This is a delightful game for a rainy day, and the preparations for it are very simple. In fact, when you have fashioned the disk of lead with a raffia covering, there is nothing to provide but a piece of chalk. You can buy, from almost any plumber or tinsmith, for a few cents, a scrap of sheet lead two or three inches square and about as thick as a half dollar. Upon this piece of lead lay a half dollar, draw around it with a pencil and cut out the circle with a sharp, strong pair of scissors. It cuts as easily as cardboard of the same thickness. Bore a hole one-quarter of an inch across through the centre of the disk with a gimlet or sharp-pointed awl. It is possible to use the disk just as it is, but it makes less noise if it is covered with raffia. To do this, thread a worsted (or tapestry) needle with raffia—the grass-like material that you have seen used for making baskets. Tie the other end of the raffia through the disk, as shown in Fig. 12 A, put the needle down through the hole in the centre, up through the loop in the raffia (see Fig. 12 B) and pull your strand up close to the edge. This will make a stitch like that shown in Fig. 12 C—what sailors call a half hitch and mothers a buttonhole stitch. Make more of these stitches around the disk, until finally it is entirely covered (see Fig. 13). If the strand of raffia gives out before the disk is covered sew the short end through the last two or three stitches on the edge of the disk and start a new piece by bringing the end through the last stitch on the edge. The short ends of both strands should be covered with the buttonhole stitches as you go on.

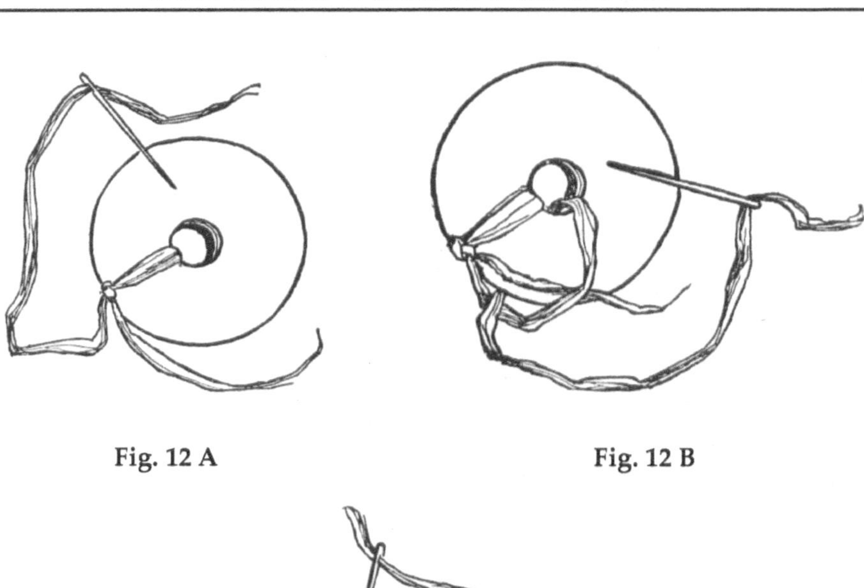

Fig. 12 A   Fig. 12 B

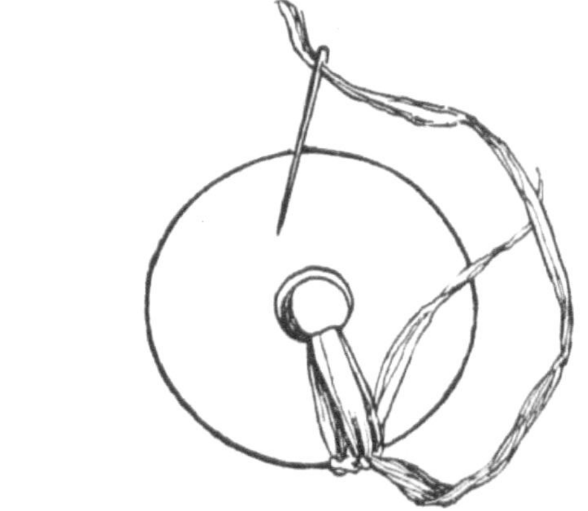

Fig. 12 C

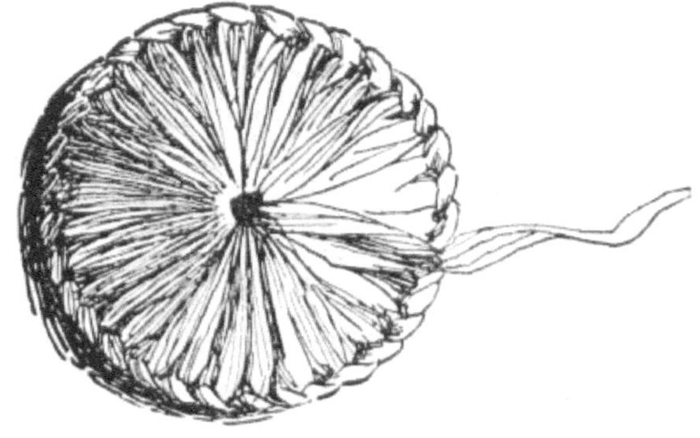

Fig. 13

Now mark the diagram shown in Fig. 14 on the playroom floor with chalk, making the diamond two feet long by a foot and a half wide. In the centre of it is a circle, four inches across, which is home. Each player takes his turn at throwing the disk, standing on a line eight feet away. If he throws the disk into the space marked 1 he counts that he has a man on first base; if on 2, that he has one on second; and if on H, a home run is counted. If by chance with his first and second throws he puts the disk into 2 and 3 and with the third throw sends it into H he will have three runs to his credit. Should he throw the disk into F he loses one point from his score, and when he has thrown the disk outside the diamond three times he is out.

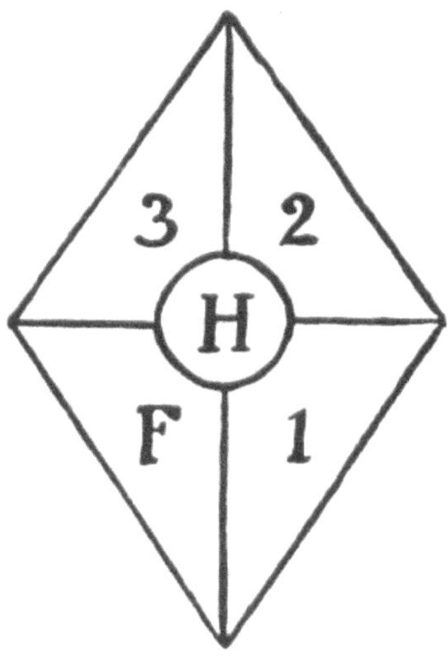

Fig. 14

A Rug for the Doll's House

Materials Required: A small wooden frame,

A piece of cream-coloured canvas,

A ball of dull green worsted,

A ball of cream white worsted,

A steel crochet needle, No. 2.

Hooked rugs such as our grandmothers used to make are great fun to do. Why should not a little girl make one of finer materials for the floor of her doll's house? Either an empty slate frame or a wooden frame such as is sold by dealers in kindergarten supplies for chair caning will do very well to hold the canvas of which the rug is made. Instead of strips of woolen we shall use worsted of various colours, and a strong steel crochet needle will be needed for "hooking."

When you have decided upon the size of the rug you wish to make cut a piece of canvas an inch wider and longer than it is to be, and make a hem a quarter of an inch wide all around it. With a needleful of white linen thread sew the rug into the frame, taking the stitches through the edge of the canvas and around the frame until it is securely fastened in. Suppose a green rug is planned, with a group of white stripes at each end. It will be well to mark on the canvas where the stripes are to run before beginning the work. The worsted should be wound into balls.

Starting with an end of the green worsted, at the lower right side of the frame, hold it under the rug and hook it up through the canvas with the crochet needle. Draw up a long enough end so that it can be cut off when the rug is finished and leave a thick texture. Do not make all the loops the same height, for if now and then one is left too low to cut with the others it will make the rug wear better. One after another of these loops is drawn through the canvas, leaving two threads of canvas between every two loops, in a straight line across the rug. When the edge of the rug is reached a row is made above the one just finished, bringing the worsted from left to right. So it goes on till the rug is finished, only changing the ball of green worsted for a white one when it is time to make the stripes. After the hooking is done, the tops of the longer loops are cut off with a sharp pair of scissors, so as to make a smooth, soft rug. It will wear better if it is lined.

When you have completed this rug you may want to make others with patterns woven into them. Draw the pattern on the canvas with a soft lead pencil and it will be quite easy to work.

CHAPTER III

BASKET WEAVING

The rattan of which the baby's go-cart and mother's armchair are woven came from a far-away forest in India. Troops of monkeys may have swung upon the very pieces on which your baby brother is bouncing, for the rattan hung from tree to tree in long festoons. One day some brown natives cut it down and stripped it of its leaves. It was then packed in bundles and sent to this country. The hard, shiny bark cut into strips has been woven into cane seats for chairs, and the inner part or core of the rattan was cut by a machine into the round strands that you see in wicker furniture.

It takes a man's strong hands to weave great armchairs and baby carriages, but boys and girls can make charming little mats and baskets as well as tiny chairs and tables for the doll's house, and other interesting things. Dealers in kindergarten supplies sell the rattan in different sizes, from No. 00, which is as fine as cord, to No. 7 or No. 8, which is almost as thick as rope. You will only need the medium sizes, Nos. 2, 3 and 4, for your weaving, with some raffia—the soft but strong fibre that the gardener uses for tying up his plants. This you will also find at the kindergarten-supply store. A pair of shears, a yardstick and an awl are the only tools you will need.

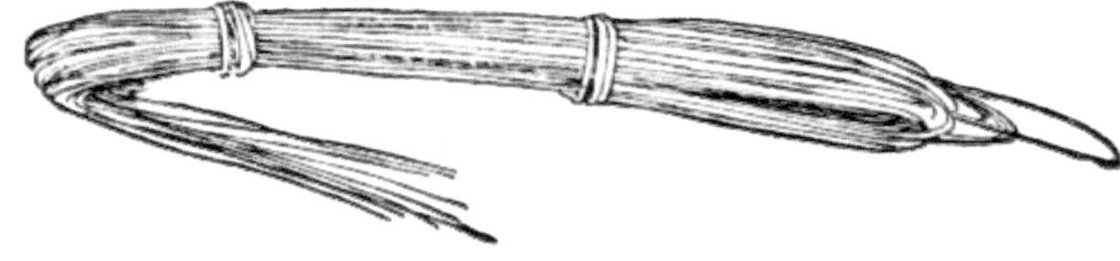

Fig. 15. Twist of Rattan

Rattan comes in long skeins or twists (see Fig. 15). Always draw it out from the loop end, so that it will not get tangled and break. Two sizes of rattan are generally used in making a basket, the thicker for the spokes or ribs and the fine for the weavers. Both must be soaked in warm water to make them soft and pliable.

As many spokes as are needed are first cut the required length and tied together with a piece of raffia. The weavers are then coiled into rings, so that they also can be soaked. This is done as follows: Starting near one end of a length of rattan, coil it into a ring. Twist the short end around this ring once or twice to hold it (see Fig. 16). Coil the rest of the strand into rings, one above the other, and twist the other end of the rattan around them all until they are held securely. Have ready a basin or pail of warm water—not hot—and let the spokes and weaver soak in it for ten or fifteen minutes.

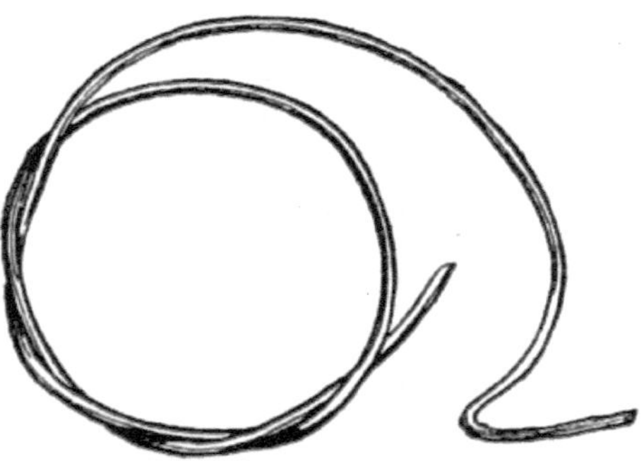

Fig. 16

Suppose we begin with a mat, which is started, just as the baskets are, at the centre.

A Mat or Stand for a Teapot

Materials Required: 4 12-inch spokes of No. 4 rattan,

1 7-inch spoke of No. 4 rattan,

1 weaver of No. 2 rattan.

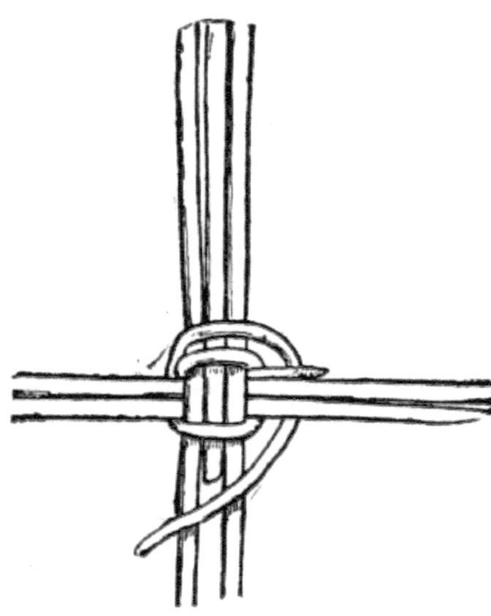

Fig. 17

Feel the ends of your weavers and you will find that some are stiff while others are almost as soft and pliable as cord. Choose a soft one to start the mat. The four spokes arranged in pairs are crossed in the centre, the vertical ones being above the others, or nearer to you. Place the short spoke, seven inches long, between the upper parts of these vertical spokes. They are held in position by the left hand, which is, as always, the one that holds, while the right is the weaving hand. An end of the weaver (which has first been unwound) is placed along the horizontal spokes, back of the vertical ones, with its tip toward the right. The forefinger of the right hand now presses the weaver across the vertical spokes and down behind the horizontal ones on the right (thus binding the end of the weaver securely), next over the lower vertical spokes and behind the horizontal ones on the left (see Fig. 17). This is repeated, and then, starting with the upper vertical spokes, the spokes are separated and the weaving begins (see Fig. 18). If you want to do close, even work, do not pull the rattan as you weave, but *press* it with the forefinger, under and over the spokes as close to the work as possible. The spokes should be very evenly separated, for upon this much of the beauty and strength of your baskets will depend. Think of the regular spaces between the spokes of a wheel and how much trouble one badly placed spoke would make. When there is just enough weaver left to go around once, the edge is bound off. This is very much like overcasting.

Fig. 18

After going under one spoke and over another, the weaver is passed under the last row of weaving just before it reaches the next spoke. It then goes behind that spoke, in front of the next and under the last row of weaving before the next spoke. When a row of this binding has been made around the edge the mat is finished with the following border: Cut the spokes all the same length, not straight across but slanting, so as to make a point that can easily be pushed down between the weaving. Then hold them in water for a few minutes. When they are quite pliable the first spoke (any one you choose to begin with) is pushed down between the rows of weaving beside the one to the left of it or spoke No. 2. No. 2 is pushed down beside the next one to the left, No. 3, and so on all the way around the mat. Take care that at least an inch of each spoke is pressed below the edge of the mat.

Basket Weaving

Small Candy Basket

Materials Required: 4 14-inch spokes of No. 4 rattan,

1 8-inch spoke of No. 4 rattan,

2 weavers of No. 2 rattan.

This little basket may be woven of rattan in the natural colour and afterward dyed or gilded, or one can buy the rattan already coloured.

Weave a bottom like the beginning of the mat, and when it measures two inches in diameter (that is, from side to side, across the centre), wet the spokes and turn them up. The spokes should be turned up away from you, for the side toward the person weaving is always the outside of the basket and the weaving should go from left to right—as you read. Bend them over the middle finger so that the sides of the basket will be curved.

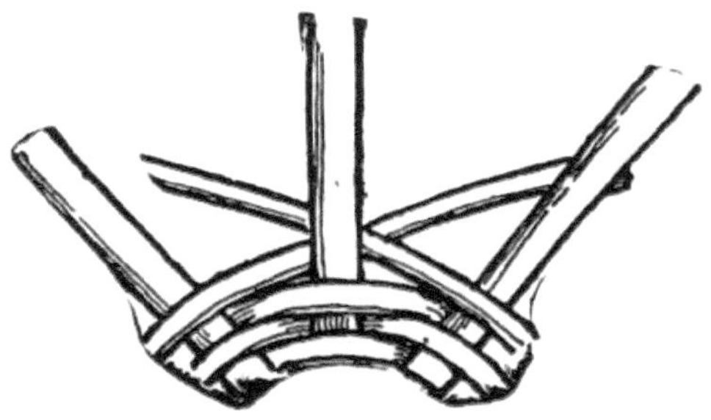

Fig. 19. Joining Weavers

Place the bottom of the basket on your knee, with the side which in starting was toward you turned down and the spokes bent upward, and do the weaving of the sides in that position. In joining a new weaver lay it across the end of the old one, back of a spoke (see Fig. 19).

The weaver at first should not be drawn too tight, but allowed to go easily, though it must be pressed closely down upon the row beneath it. When about three-quarters of an inch has been woven up the sides, the spokes are drawn gradually closer together by a slight tightening of the weaver, and this should be continued until an inch more has been woven. Bind off and finish with this border. The spokes for the border should measure at least four inches from the last row of weaving to the end of the spoke. Cut and soak as described in the directions for making a mat. Spoke No. 1 crosses the next one on the left, or No. 2, and is pushed down beside the next spoke, No. 3. No. 2 crosses No. 3 and is pushed down beside No. 4, and so on around the basket.

Doll's Table of Rattan

Materials Required: 6 22-inch spokes of No. 3 rattan,

1 12-inch spoke of No. 3 rattan,

1 weaver of No. 2 rattan,

A piece of fine wire, 4 or 5 inches long,

Several strands of raffia,

An awl.

Perhaps you did not think it was as interesting to make a mat as to weave baskets, but you will be glad you know how to do it when you see some of the things that can be made with mats. For example, this dear little wicker table, just the size for a doll's house and the shape for an afternoon tea.

Two groups of spokes, one of three and the other of three and a half, are crossed in the centre. The short spoke should be put between two others, never on the outside of a group. The mat is woven like the other mat and basket until it is three and a half inches in diameter, when the edge is bound off. Bring each spoke across the next one and press it down beside the next, as in the border of the basket, except that the long end is not cut off, but brought out between the fourth and fifth rows of weaving on the under side of the mat. The loops of the border are drawn in so that they will not be more than a quarter of an inch beyond the weaving. The long ends of the spokes (which are to form the legs of the table) are brought together and bound with a piece of fine wire just under the centre. Separate them into three groups of four spokes each. The odd spoke is either cut off or whittled very thin and bound in with one of the three groups. A strand of raffia is now doubled around two or three spokes, above the wire binding, and wound tightly around one of the groups until it has covered two inches, from the binding down. At the end a half hitch or one buttonhole stitch is made, to keep the raffia from slipping. It is then wound up again to the top. The raffia is brought down the second leg as far as the first one was wound; here it is turned with a half hitch and brought up again in the same way. The third leg is also wound down and up again, with a half hitch at the bottom to hold it. After this third leg has been covered the raffia is brought in and out between the legs, where they separate, in order to spread them more. It is then tied and the ends are cut close. Finally the spokes at the end of each leg are cut slanting so that the table will stand firmly.

Doll's Chair of Rattan

Materials Required: 6 20-inch spokes of No. 3 rattan,

1 11-inch spoke of No. 3 rattan,

4 10-inch spokes of No. 3 rattan,

1 piece of No. 3 rattan about 9 inches long,

2 weavers of No. 2 rattan,

Several strands of raffia,

An awl.

Would you like to make a tiny high-backed chair to use with the tea table in the doll's house? It is only a trifle more difficult to make than the table.

Two groups of twenty-inch spokes of No. 3 rattan, one having three and the other three and a half spokes in it, are crossed at the centre, bound around twice with a weaver of No. 2 rattan and woven into a mat three inches in diameter. After binding off the edge the following border is made: Each spoke is brought down beside the next one, as in the border of the mat, except that the long end is drawn out between the second and third rows of weaving on the under side of the mat. When all the spokes have been brought out in this way underneath the mat, or seat, the four groups of three spokes each which are to form the legs are so divided that the vertical spokes in the centre of the chair seat shall run toward the front and back of the seat. The thirteenth spoke is whittled to a thin point and bound in with one of the other groups, which are wound with raffia down to the end, turned with a half hitch and brought up again. A neat way to start the raffia is to thread it across a row of weaving in the chair seat, just above the group it is to bind.

A piece of No. 3 rattan about nine inches long is coiled into a ring and held within the space enclosed by the legs, about half way down, where it is wound around with a strand of raffia and bound securely to each leg.

The back of the chair is formed by inserting four spokes of No. 3 rattan, ten inches long, beside those in the seat, at that part of the seat which has been chosen for the back. To do this push a sharp pointed awl in between the weaving, beside a spoke, draw it out and you will have made room for the new spoke to run in. Bend the spokes up and weave back and forth upon them with a No. 2 weaver, turning on the outside spokes. Needless to say, the weaver must be very soft and pliable in order to make these sharp turns. You will find that you can make almost any kind of a back you choose.

If you decide to make an oval-shaped back, then when you have woven it high enough, bring each of the outside spokes over and down beside the other one, running it in between the weaving. The inner spokes are crossed at the centre and run down beside the outer spokes. To make an armchair insert six spokes instead of four at the back of the seat and weave the outer spokes in with the others for a few rows. They are then bent over and forward to form the arms. Each is cut to the desired length and run in beside one of the side spokes in the seat.

A Bird's Nest

Materials Required: 8 18-inch spokes of No. 3 rattan,

1 10-inch spoke of No. 3 rattan,

1 ½ weavers of No. 2 rattan,

A bunch of raffia

A tapestry needle, No. 18.

At the Bird Market in Paris charming little nests are sold, woven of rushes on spokes of brown twigs, in the shape of an Indian tepee. They are intended for caged birds, who cannot build their own nests of sticks and grass and horsehair from the fields and wayside. Some free birds like them, too—wrens, for example.

A boy or girl who has made the mat and basket and doll's furniture will have no difficulty in weaving one of these nests. Then there will be the delight of hanging it in a tree (not too near the house) and watching to see what bird will choose it when nesting time comes.

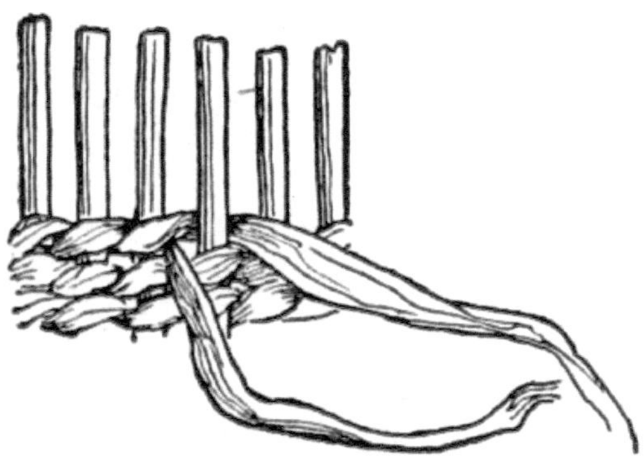

Fig. 20

Let us weave a nest that shall be light and yet firm. Spokes of rattan will give it strength and weavers of raffia will make it soft and comfortable. Two groups of spokes, one of four and the other of four and a half, are crossed at the centre, bound three times with a strand of raffia and woven into a bottom an inch and a half across. Another weaver is then added and an inch of pairing is made. Pairing, or *bam tush*, as the Indians call it, is a simple stitch. Two weavers are started, each one behind a spoke (see Fig. 20). The one on the left is brought over the first spoke, under the next and down in front. It is now the turn of the second weaver, which also passes over the first spoke on its right, under the next and outside, where it is held down in front while the other weaver repeats the process. So it goes on around the nest. The spokes are then wet so that the bottom may be formed into a bowl shape, with sides rounding up from the very centre. A row of pairing in No. 2 rattan is next woven to hold the slippery raffia in place. This is followed by five-eighths of an inch of raffia woven in pairing, the sides still being flared. Two rows of pairing in No. 2 rattan are then woven, drawing the spokes in very slightly. At this point, which is the widest, the nest should measure eleven inches around the top. A row of under and over weaving is started, and at the place which has been chosen for the doorway the weaver is doubled back on a spoke and woven from right to left until it comes to the second spoke to the right of the one it first doubled around. It is brought around this spoke, thus making the beginning of a doorway, which has an unused spoke in the centre of it. The weaver then returns to the spoke it first doubled around, where it doubles back again. This is repeated until the doorway is an inch and a quarter high. Two rows of pairing in No. 2 rattan are then woven all the way around, forming a firm top for the doorway, where they cross it. The spokes are drawn in closer and closer with rows of pairing in raffia, until, when an inch and a half has been woven, they meet at the top. The ends of the spokes are left uneven lengths and bound around with a strand of raffia threaded through a tapestry needle.

A loop to hang it by is made of two strands of raffia, five and a half inches long, covered close with buttonhole stitch in raffia. The spoke in the centre of the doorway should be cut at the lower part of the opening, just above the weaving, and after it has been wet until quite pliable it is bent and pressed up between the weaving beside the upper part of the same spoke.

CHAPTER IV

KNOTS WITH RAFFIA AND CORD

Sailors' knots are of course fascinating to boys, but why should not girls enjoy making them, too? Think of the dolls' hammocks, the work bags and twine ball nets one can make, and think of being able to tie a good, square knot—one that will hold—instead of the "granny knots" that brothers and boy cousins laugh at!

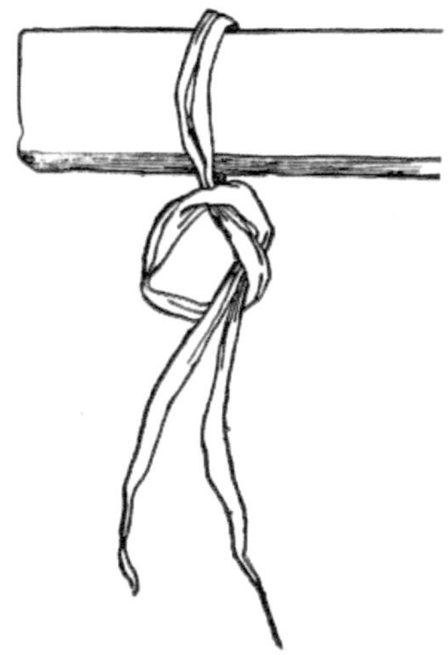

Fig. 21

Of course you know how to tie the simplest knot of all—the one shown in Fig. 21. Let us call it the loop knot, for it is made by tying the ends of a strand together to form a loop. You have used it often for that purpose, I am sure, and sometimes to tie two pieces of string together. You can make a pretty and useful sponge bag of raffia in the natural colour with this knot. The wet sponge will not hurt the raffia, and in such an open bag the air soon dries it.

Knotted Sponge Bag

Materials Required: 25 strands of raffia,

A length of No. 5 rattan,

A tapestry needle.

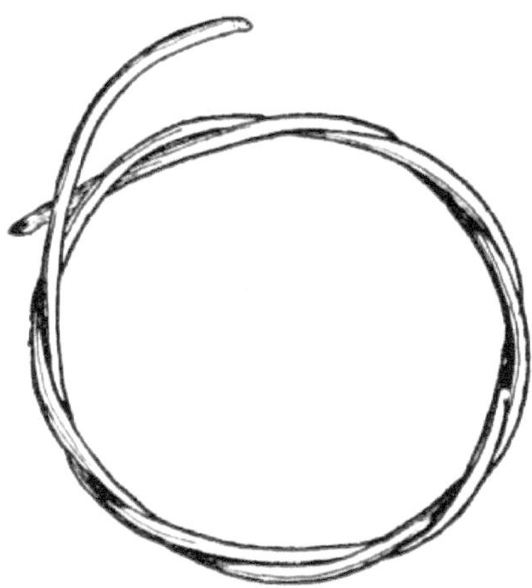

Fig. 22

Roll a length of No. 5 rattan into a ring, as described on page 38, so that it can be soaked in warm water till it is pliable. Cut it into three pieces, each forty-seven inches long. Tie an end of one of these pieces into a ring seven inches in diameter and twist the long end in and out once around this (see Fig. 22). At the end of this row the ends, where they meet, should overlap an inch. If they are longer, cut them off with a slanting cut and tie them tightly together with a piece of raffia. Two more rings, the same size as the first one, are made with the other pieces of rattan. Hang one of the rings where you can reach it easily, on a low bedpost, for example. Double a strand of raffia and tie it through the ring as shown in Fig. 21, drawing the knot up quite close. Twenty-two strands are knotted on in this way. Space them along the ring about an inch apart, and, beginning with any pair of strands, tie the right-hand one with the nearest strand of the next pair on the right, making an even mesh at an inch from the first row of knots. Continue this all around the ring, when you will have made one row. Ten more rows are knotted in this way. Then bring the ends of all the strands straight down together and tie them below the centre of the ring with a piece of raffia. The ends are cut off evenly at about two inches and a half from where they were tied, to form a tassel.

The two other rings are used for the handles of the bag. Lay one of them against the ring at the top of the bag so that the places where the rings are tied will come together. Thread a tapestry needle with raffia and bind the rings together with buttonhole stitch for an inch. Then sew through and through the binding to make it secure and cut the end close to the ring. The other ring handle is bound to the opposite side of the top ring in the same way.

A Doll's Hammock

Materials Required: 14 strands of raffia,

A tapestry needle.

Even simpler to make than the sponge bag is a doll's hammock of raffia. It is knotted in just the same way.

Fig. 23

Lay twelve strands of raffia evenly together. Bend them to find the middle, or "middle them," as the sailors say. Lay the short end of another piece of raffia on the middle of the twelve strands, with its tip turning toward the left, and wind the long end round and round from right to left, binding them together for two and three-quarter inches. Bring the two ends of this binding together to form a loop, wind a strand of raffia tightly around them (see Fig. 23), and tie the ends securely. You will then have twenty-four ends to knot together, two and two, as the knots in the bag were made. Pin the loop on the cushion of a chair or tie it to a low hook or to the doorknob, so that you can pull the strands taut. The first row of knots is tied about two inches from the loop and after that the rows are only an inch apart. The finishing of the edge of the hammock is of course different from the bag.

Fig. 24

It is done in this way: In starting the second row of knots the left strand in the first pair is of course left untied, and, after knotting the row across, the right strand of the last pair is also left free. When the third row is started the loose strand on the left side of the hammock is knotted in with the left one in the first pair of strands in this row (see Fig. 24). In other words, the strands which are left untied at each side of the hammock when the second, fourth, sixth and all the even numbered rows have been knotted, are tied in with the outside strands in the next uneven numbered row. To make a hammock for a little doll thirteen rows of knotting will be enough. When the last row has been tied bring the ends of the strands together, start a new strand at two inches from the last row of knots, and bind the ends together tightly for two and three-quarter inches to make a loop like the one at the other end. After the loop is finished cut the ends close to the binding, and with a tapestry needle threaded in the end of the binding strand sew it through and through, to secure it, and cut its end close to the binding.

How to Tie a Square or Reef Knot

Fig. 25

Once upon a time a little girl was carrying a bundle of cookies by the string, when suddenly the knot slipped and the cookies rolled in every direction, over the sidewalk and into the street. If the baker's wife had known how to tie a square knot instead of that useless "granny," the accident would never have happened. I wonder if you have ever had an experience of this kind. If so, I am sure you will like to learn how to tie the ends of a piece of string together so that they cannot slip.

Fig. 26

Take the ends of a piece of string, one in each hand. Cross them and bring the upper end down under the long end of the other piece (see Fig. 25). Now turn it back in the opposite direction above the first part of the knot, to make a loop, and pass the other end down through it (see Fig. 26). In this way each end of the string will come out beside its own beginning.

Two Hitches

There is no simple knot that you will find more useful than the half hitch. It is described in the directions for making the game of Floor Baseball in Chapter II. Two of these half hitches, side by side, are called by sailors a "clove hitch." In making nets this clove hitch is used to attach the first row of meshes to the top line or head rope, as it is called.

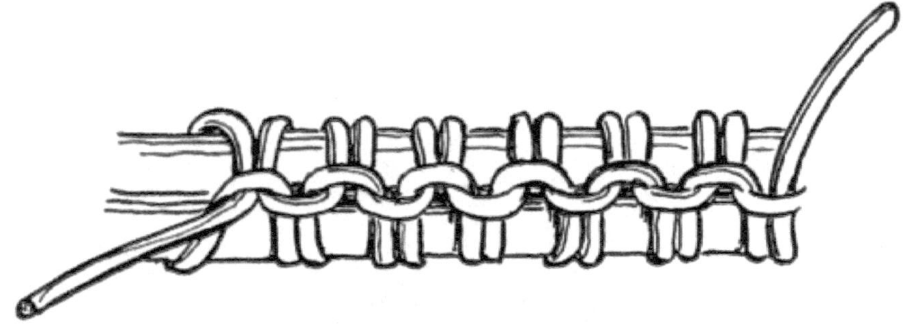

Fig. 27

Another use for the half hitch is in the process that sailors call "kackling" (see Fig. 27). This is used to prevent two ropes from rubbing against one another, or chafing. A beautiful handle for a basket or bag may be made with this knot.

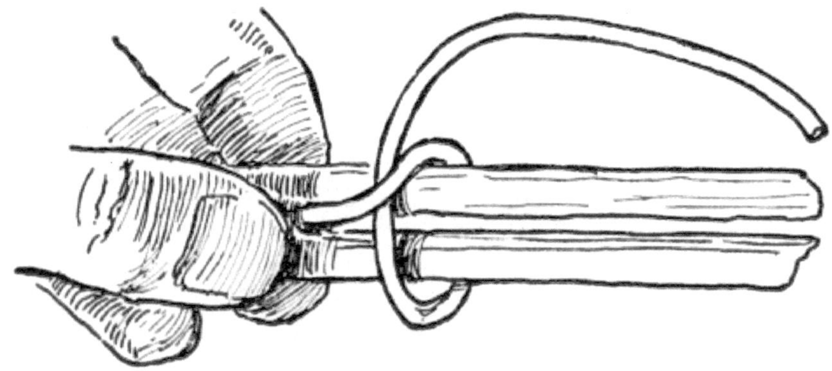

Fig. 28

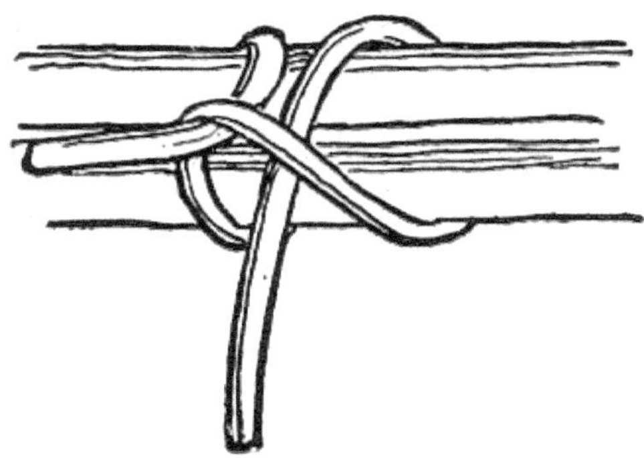

Fig. 29

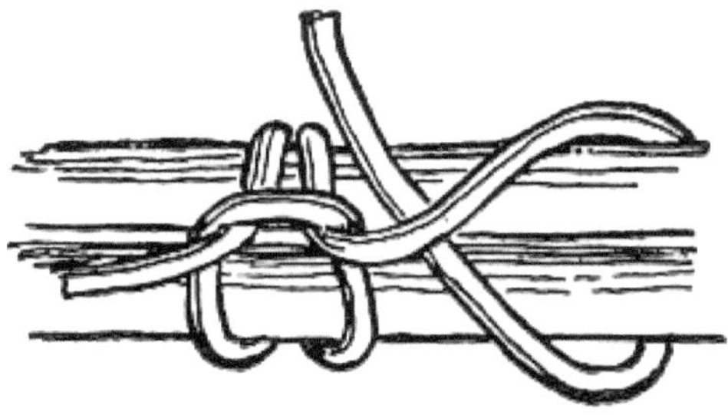

Fig. 30

Take two pieces of rope and some light cord, or, if it is to be the handle of a basket, two pieces of heavy rattan, No. 5, and some No. 00 rattan with which to do the knotting. If you use the rattan be sure to soak it for ten minutes in warm water and choose a soft piece of the fine rattan for knotting. Hold the heavy pieces of rattan side by side, lay an end of the fine rattan upon them at the middle (see Fig. 28), with its tip turning toward the left, and hold it there with the left hand, while with the right you bring the long end up and around both of the large pieces of rattan up and under the short end of the fine piece. It is then brought down and around the two large pieces of rattan and the end is passed down through the loop made in starting the hitch (see Fig. 29). Draw the tying strand up tight and bring the long end up and around the large pieces of rattan and up under the loop it left in starting (see Fig. 30). Take care to keep the fine rattan wet so that it will be very pliable; if it dries it will surely crack as you tie it.

Net Making

If you would like to make a ping-pong net or a net for crabbing, you will find it quite easy to do and very interesting. After you have made these small nets you may feel like trying a tennis net if you have plenty of time and patience.

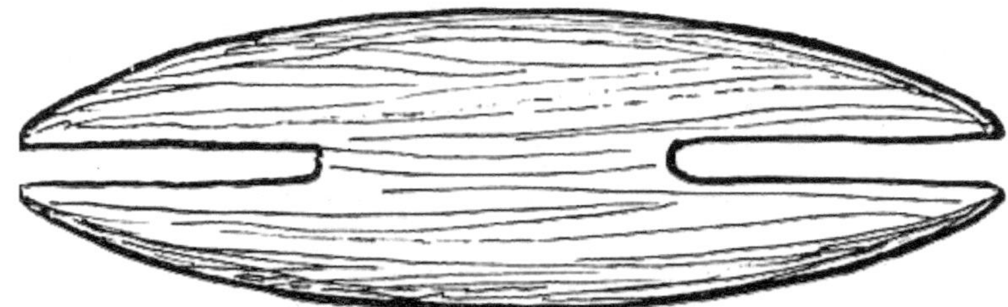

Fig. 31

At a hardware store you can buy tightly twisted cord of the size you wish to use in making your net. It is generally sold by weight. If you are planning to make a ping-pong or tennis net you will also need a heavy piece of cord for the head rope. A crab net would of course be netted on to an iron ring attached to a long wooden handle. A needle such as is shown in Fig. 31 may be made quite easily by any boy who can whittle.

Fig. 32

When you have wound your cord on the needle, stretch the head rope taut between two convenient points, the backs of two chairs, for example, and begin at the left by tying one end of the cord to it. Make a loop the size you wish the mesh to be and fasten the cord to the head rope with a clove hitch, or two half hitches (see Fig. 32). When you have worked as far as you wish, get on the other side of the net and work back again. This row of meshes and all that follow after are made by fastening them to the upper row with a sheet bend (see Fig. 32). After the second row is finished come around to the other side again and knot the third row. When the net is wide enough knot it to a piece of rope the size of the head rope with a row of clove hitches.

The Weaver's Knot

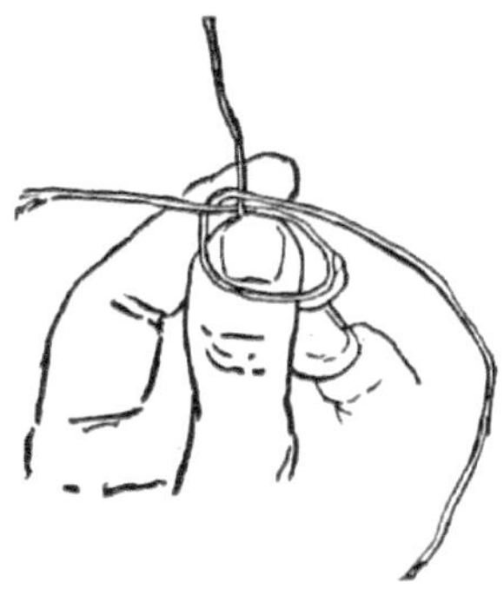

Fig. 33

In weaving bead chains on a loom, and in doing other things, you will often need to tie a new piece of thread or cord to a very short end. The weavers have a knot they use for this purpose, and as it is a simple one perhaps you would like to learn it. Hold the old end in a vertical position (that is, as if it were standing up), lay the new piece back of it, its short end turning toward the left and reaching an inch or more beyond the vertical thread. Bring the long end around in front of the vertical thread, up back of its own short end on the left and across in front of the vertical thread (see Fig. 33). All these threads are held in position by the fingers and thumbs of the left hand, while the right hand brings the thread around. The vertical or old end is now turned down through the loop in front of it and there held by the thumb, while with the fingers of both hands the long and short ends of the new thread are pulled up tight.

Turk's Head

There is a beautiful knot called by sailors a "Turk's head." Girls will find that they can make the prettiest buttons imaginable with it, using silk cord of any colour, and both boys and girls will enjoy making napkin rings of rattan with a more open arrangement of the same knot.

Fig. 34

Fig. 35

To make a button take a yard of cord, and at about four inches from one end bend it into a loop (like the one shown in Fig. 34), about half an inch across. The long end should come above the short one. Next make a second loop lying above and to the left of the first one (see Fig. 35), bringing the long end under the short one left in starting. The long end is then brought over the left side of the second loop, under the left side of the first loop, over the right side of the second loop, under the right side of the first and around to the beginning, inside of the short end (see Fig. 36). This makes one row, or the beginning of the button. If you have a bodkin with a large eye, the long end of the cord can be threaded into it and this will make the work easier. The next row follows the first one exactly—close to it and always on the inside. When the cord has followed in this way four times, to complete four rows (keeping the button form always in mind and moulding the cord into that shape), a firm little button will have been made.

Fig. 36

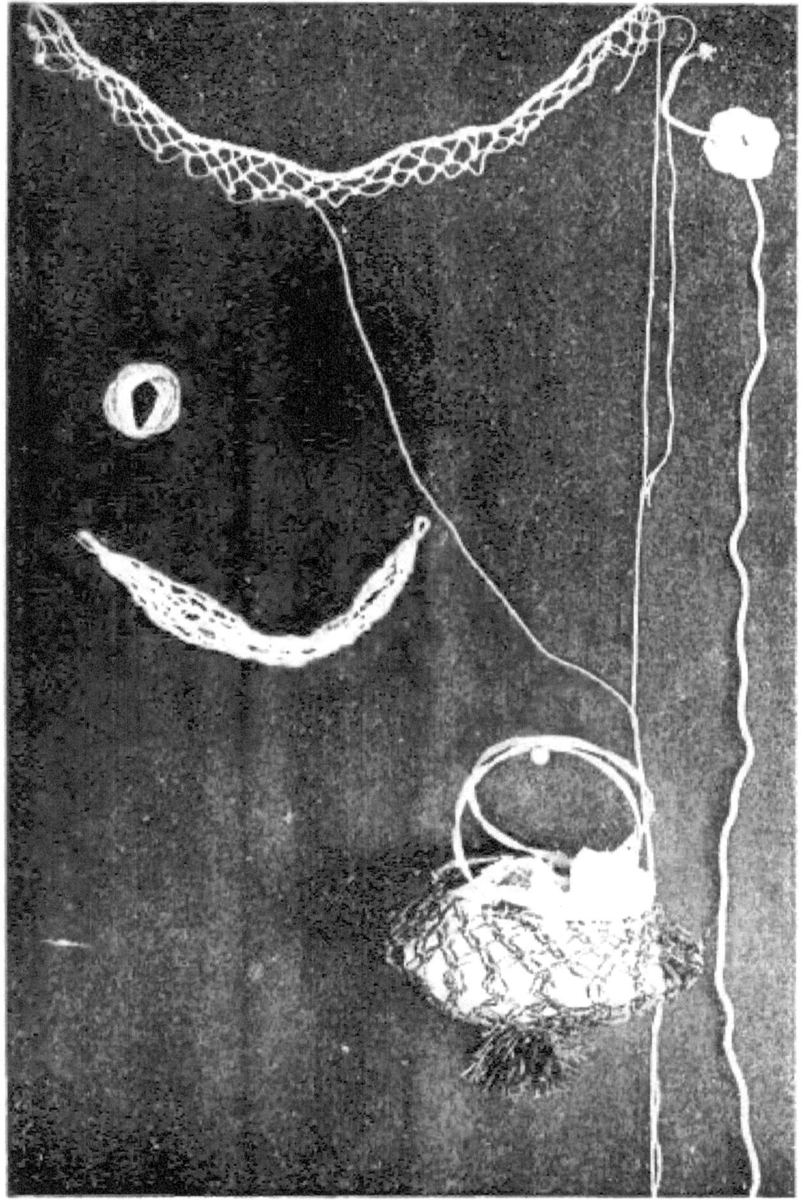

Knots with Raffia and Cord:
1. The beginning of a ping pong net. 2. A Turk's-head knot.
3. Raffia work bag. 4. Doll's hammock. 5. A rattan napkin ring

At the top of the plate is the beginning of a ping-pong net. Below it at
the right is the Turk's-head knot. Still lower the knotted raffia work bag

hangs. On the left is swung a doll's hammock of knotted raffia and above it a rattan napkin ring, made with the Turk's-head knot

Napkin Ring

Material Required: 1 length of No. 4 rattan.

With a piece of rattan in the natural colour or a length of coloured rattan you can make a useful and very pretty napkin ring by following the directions just given, with only one change. In beginning the second row (shown in Fig. 36), the long end is brought to the left or outside of the short end and continues around on that side. Five rows may be made instead of four. Keep the ring form in mind all the time, have the rattan wet and pliable and mould it into the shape of a ring, keeping the top and bottom as nearly the same size as possible.

Green Raffia Work Bag

Materials Required: A bunch of green raffia,

A length of No. 5 green rattan,

A tapestry needle.

A Tapestry Needle

When your mother was a little girl her mother used to make with linen twine a kind of coarse, heavy lace called macramé. One of the knots she used was called "Solomon's knot," and that is the one you will use if you decide to make this work bag. A length of No. 4 rattan and a bunch of raffia, both in a soft shade of green, will be needed. These you can buy of a dealer in basket materials for a few cents. Twist three rings like those for the upper edge and handles of the sponge bag described in the first part of this chapter. Hang one of these rings on a low bedpost or on a hook placed so that you can reach it easily when seated. Take two strands of raffia, double them around the ring, and with the four ends thus made tie a Solomon's knot as follows: Hold the two upper strands straight and taut. Bend the under strand on the left across them to the right (see Fig. 37), and bring the under strand on the right over the end of the left strand, back of the middle strands and through the loop made by the left strand in starting. Another pair of strands is knotted on in the same way, and another, until there are twenty-two groups around the ring. Starting anywhere on the ring, the two strands on the right of a group are brought beside the two on the left of the next group to the right. The middle pair of these four strands are held straight down, while the strands on the right and left are tied upon them in a Solomon's knot. This knot should be half an inch from those in the first row. Make a double knot this time as follows: After tying the knot (shown in Fig. 37), take the end which is on the right after the first knot has tied, bring it over to the left, above the middle strands, and bring the one on the left down over the end of the strand which was on the right, back of the two middle strands and up through the loop left in starting the right strand (see Fig. 38). The whole row is made in this way. Ten rows are knotted, each one about half an inch from the row above. The bag is finished in the same way as the sponge bag, with a tassel and two handles. If you choose you can line it with silk of the same colour as the raffia, or, if it is to be used for a duster bag or to hold grandmother's knitting, it will not need a lining.

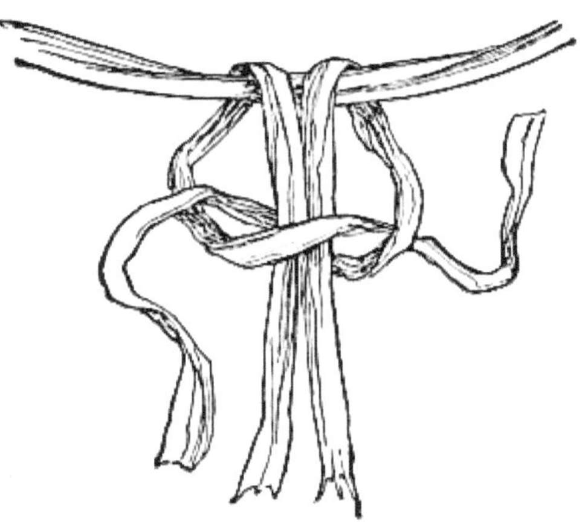

Fig. 37

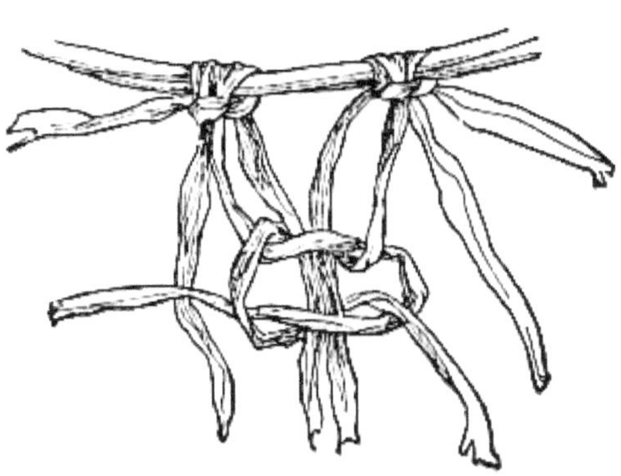

Fig. 38

CHAPTER V
WHAT A CHILD CAN DO WITH BEADS

Long, long ago when the world was young, the child who wished for a gay and pretty necklace for her little brown throat strung berries and seeds or pieces of shell and bone that her father ground smooth by hand and pierced for stringing. For thread there were grasses and fibres of plants or sinews of deer.

Indian children sometimes used beads of clay, and so did the little Egyptians, for the fine clay by the river Nile made beautiful beads, as well as pottery. The children of the North—the little Esquimaux—had beads of amber, and the Indian tribes farther south strung shells that look so much like the teeth of animals one can hardly believe they are anything else. Look for them at the Natural History Museum and you will see that this is so.

Nowadays there are of course many more kinds of beads—beads of glass, china, gold and silver, and even of semi-precious stones. After all, though, the child who lives in the country or by the sea can gather the most interesting kind of all—such as were strung by those children who lived so long ago—seeds, berries, shells and seaweed. Gather them on a sunshiny day and store them away for use in the dull hours when you are obliged to be indoors.

The seeds of muskmelons are soft enough to pierce; watermelon seeds will take more effort and a stronger needle. Then there are the orange berries of bittersweet and the red ones of holly. Haws or hawthorn berries are a beautiful red, too, and perhaps you will find in a neighbour's garden a bush of Job's tears—gray, white or brown. The grape-like seaweed which bursts with a pop when you step on it makes very pretty beads. Cut each one close to the bulb, yet far enough to leave a short piece of the stem on each side of the bead. Pierce the bulbs while they are still wet, and after they have dried for a few days they will be ready to string. Apple and flax seeds, beans and peas before they have dried, make excellent beads. A few of the small glass beads which come in bunches may be used with these natural beads, and will set them off wonderfully. Although they are usually sold in bunches, eight skeins to a bunch, the skeins can sometimes be bought separately. Olive-green crystal beads of the size that dealers call No. 3-0 are beautiful with red berries, and what could be prettier to string with brown seeds or Job's tears than gold-lined crystal beads? Let us use them in making a chain for a muff or fan.

Muff Chain in Brown and Gold

Materials Required: 12 brown seeds or Job's tears,

A bunch of gold-lined crystal beads, No. 3-0,

A spool of No. 60 white linen thread,

A No. 5 needle.

Have you ever seen any Job's tears—the interesting tear-shaped seeds of an East Indian grass? It grows very well in this climate, and you may like to raise it yourself. Think of being able to pick beads from a plant of your own!

Be careful to boil these beads before stringing, for a little grub sometimes lives in them, and he may appear when you least expect him or may even make a meal of the thread on which the beads are strung. If you have not the Job's tears, apple seeds will look almost as well, or you can buy at the grocer's whole allspice. Use a No. 5 needle and a piece of No. 60 white linen thread four inches longer than you wish the chain to be when it is finished; two yards and a quarter is a good length.

String a seed and draw it down to the middle of the thread, then string some of the gold-lined crystal beads for about three-quarters of an inch. A seed is next threaded on, and then quarter of an inch of gold-lined beads. Keep on in this way, first threading a seed and then quarter of an inch of gold-lined beads, until there are only two inches of the thread left. Tie this end through a bead to keep the others from slipping off. Thread your needle with the other end of the strand and start by stringing three-quarters of an inch of the gold-lined beads, then a seed and quarter of an inch of gold-lined beads. When this end of the strand has been strung—just as the other was—to within two inches of the tip, tie the two ends together and the chain is finished.

Raffia and Bead Chain

Materials Required: 2 strands of rose-pink raffia,

A bunch of large rose-pink crystal beads,

2 fine darning needles.

Another pretty and simple chain is made of large rose-pink crystal beads strung on pink raffia; or you can use seeds or berries instead of the crystal beads, in which case the raffia will have to be split. Tie the strands of raffia together at one end, and on each of the other ends thread a fine darning needle. String one bead, then pass both needles through a single bead and through another and another (see Fig. 38a). Two beads are then slipped on each strand (see Fig. 38a). Next both needles pass through three beads, and so on to the end of the chain. Tie the ends securely.

Double Chain of Seeds and Beads

Materials Required: A bunch of crystal beads, letter E,

25 large beads of a deeper shade or the same number of seeds or berries,

A spool of No. 60 white linen thread,

A No. 5 needle.

A double chain like the one shown in Fig 39 may be made of crystal E beads strung with seeds or larger beads of a deeper shade. Measure off a piece of white linen thread, No. 60, double the length you wish the chain to be. Three yards twenty-two inches will make a chain sixty-five inches long, which is a good size. In one end of it thread a No. 5 needle and string one large bead, or seed, which should be pushed down to the middle of the strand. Here it may be tied, to hold it in place. Next string two inches and a half of E beads, then another large bead, or seed, and so on to the end of the strand, where the tip is tied through the last bead. The other end of the strand is then threaded and two inches and a half of the E beads are strung, the needle passes through the next large bead on the end first strung (see Fig 39), and two and a half inches more of the E beads are threaded. So it goes on to the end of the chain—the needle always passing through the next large bead on the strand already strung, after two inches and a half of E beads have been threaded.

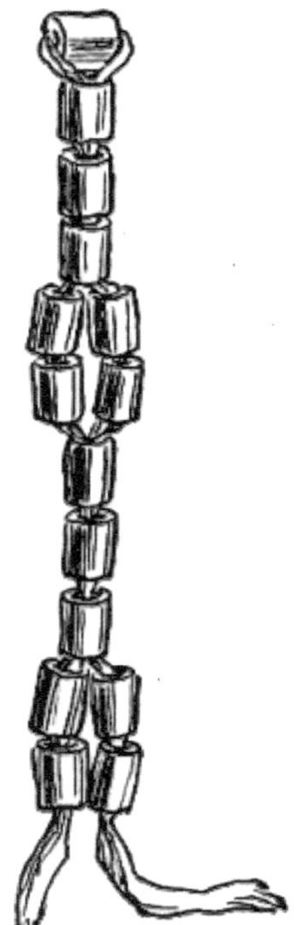

Fig. 38 A

Fig. 39

Braided Raffia Chain

Materials Required: 3 strands of pale green raffia,

66 darker green crystal beads, No. 0.

Fig. 40

A braided raffia chain with a cluster of three crystal beads every few inches is so simple that any little girl can make it. Choose pale green raffia and beads of a deeper shade, and it will look like clover leaves on their stems. String twenty-two of the green crystal beads, No. 0 size, on a strand of split raffia. On two other strands thread the same number of beads. Tie the thin end of each piece around the last bead, so that it cannot slip off. The other ends are all tied together. Now pin the knot securely to a cushion, or tie it to a hook at a convenient height and braid the three strands together closely and evenly for about two inches. Then slip a bead from each piece up close to the work and braid it in as shown in Fig. 40. This will make a clover leaf. After braiding two inches more slip another bead on each strand up close to the work and make another leaf. When it is finished tie the ends together securely.

A Daisy Chain

Materials Required: Half a bunch of olive green opaque beads, No. 3-0,

Half a bunch of milk white beads, No. 0,

1 skein yellow crystal E beads,

A spool of No. 60 white linen thread,

A No. 5 needle.

Fig. 41

Next best to making a daisy chain out-of-doors is to string one of beads. And this rainy-day chain will last as many months as the real chain would hours. First string sixteen green beads, then eight white ones. Run the needle down through the first white bead and string a yellow one. Next pass the needle through the fifth white bead (see Fig. 41) and draw the thread up tightly. This makes a daisy. String another stem of sixteen green beads and make a daisy as you did the first one. The whole chain is strung in this way.

Chain of Watermelon Seeds Strung With Beads

Materials Required: 120 fresh watermelon seeds,

A bunch of pink crystal E beads,

A spool of No. 60 white linen thread,

A No. 5 needle.

Fig. 42

A chain that is very pretty and effective may be made with watermelon seeds and pink crystal E beads, the colour of the inside of a watermelon. The seeds can be pierced quite easily with a No. 5 needle. Take two pieces of white linen thread, well waxed, the length you wish the chain to be, and two needles. Tie an E bead on the end of each piece of thread. Lay them side by side and string four more E beads on the strand at the right. Pass the needle on the left up through the three middle beads of the five on the right strand (see Fig. 42), and string one more E bead. Next thread a seed on each strand and string the E beads in the same way. So it goes on for the whole length of the chain.

If you are fond of playing Indian and have no Indian costume, you ought to be happy. That seems a strange thing to say, but the reason is this: You can have all the fun of making a costume yourself, you can learn how to do it in the Indian way, and after it is finished it will be far more like the dress worn by Western Indians than those that are sold ready made.

Suppose we begin with the belt.

It is woven on a loom—not an Indian loom, which, as perhaps you know, was a bow strung with several strings which served as the warp threads for the belt or chain. Possibly you have a loom of your own and know how to use it; but if not you can either buy one for twenty-five or fifty cents, or, what is still better, make one yourself. A simple, good loom may be made from a cigar box.

A Home Made Bead Loom

Materials Required: An oblong cigar box, about 2 ½ inches deep,

4 small sticks of wood 2 ½ inches long and ½-inch square,

16 ½-inch screws,

6 small screw eyes,

6 tacks,

A sharp knife,

A screw driver,

A hammer,

Sand paper.

Choose a good strong cigar box, one that is quite shallow, and remove the cover. Rule a line one inch from the bottom of the box on each long side and draw a sharp knife across the line several times until the upper part separates easily from the lower without injuring it. Smooth the tops of the sides with sandpaper. Fasten each of the small sticks of wood inside a corner of the box, to strengthen it. This is how it is done. Drive one of the half-inch screws up from the bottom into the end of the stick, another into it through the side, and two, one near the top and one lower down through the end of the box, into the stick. On the outside of the box at one end six round-headed tacks are driven in a row an inch and a half from the top and about three-quarters of an inch apart. Drive six screw eyes in the same position on the opposite side. Cut a row of notches on the top of each end of the loom, about one-sixteenth of an inch apart, and deep enough to hold a thread. The loom is then ready for weaving. Chalk-white beads are much used by the bead-weaving Indians like the Sioux and Winnebagos, especially for the ground-work of their belts. Let us choose them for the background of the belt and weave the design in Indian red and blue.

Indian Bead Belt

Materials Required: 1 bunch chalk white beads, No. 3-0,

4 skeins each Indian red and dark blue beads, No. 3-0,

1 spool No. 60 white linen thread,

1 spool No. 90 white linen thread,

A No. 12 needle,

A piece of wax.

Cut twenty-two pieces of No. 60 linen thread about six inches longer than you wish your belt to be. Tie a loop at one end of each piece and slip it over the round-headed tacks at one end of the loom. Bring the long ends one at a time through twenty-two of the notches at the top of the loom and stretch them across to the notches in the opposite end. Draw them taut and tie them through the screw eyes. These make the warp threads for the belt. As you will see by the pattern, the belt is twenty-one beads wide and you have twenty-two threads. This is so that there will be a thread on each side of every bead. Thread the needle with No. 90 white linen thread. Tie one end of it to the warp thread on the left (as you hold the loom with the end on which are the screw eyes toward you). Bring the needle out to the right below the warp strands, string twenty-one white beads and press them up between the warp strands, so that one bead will come between every two threads. Run the needle back from right to left through the beads, making sure that it goes *above* the warp threads. This makes one row. The whole belt is woven in the same way, except that when the figure begins the beads should be strung according to the pattern. For example, in making the first row of the pattern shown in Fig. 43, you will string nine white beads, three Indian-red ones and nine more of the white. The next two rows will be the same, and then you will string six white beads, three Indian-red, three blue, three Indian-red, and six white. Wax the thread you weave with, so that the sharp-edged beads will not cut it. In joining new needlefuls use the weaver's knot shown on p. 66. Armlets are woven in the same way, but much wider—about forty beads wide and long enough to go around the upper part of the arm. Tie them together with strips of chamois, knotted in with the ends of the warp strands. Head bands, bracelets and chains are also woven in this way.

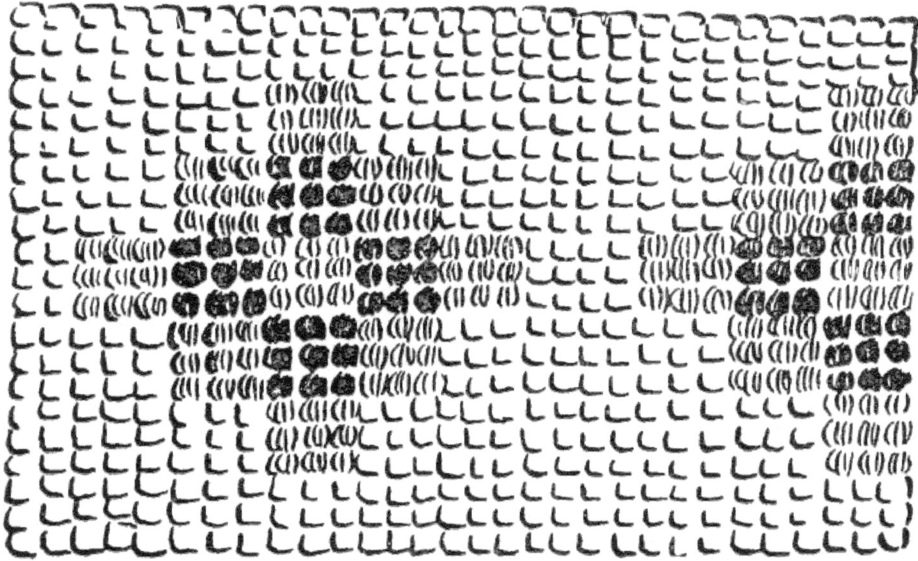

Fig. 43

Bead Wrought Indian Shirt

Materials Required: 1 large chamois skin,

2 smaller chamois skins,

1 spool white linen thread, No. 90,

A No. 11 needle,

½ bunch dark blue beads, No. 4-0,

½ bunch Indian red beads, No. 4-0,

½ bunch white opaque beads, No. 4-0,

28 large Indian red opaque beads.

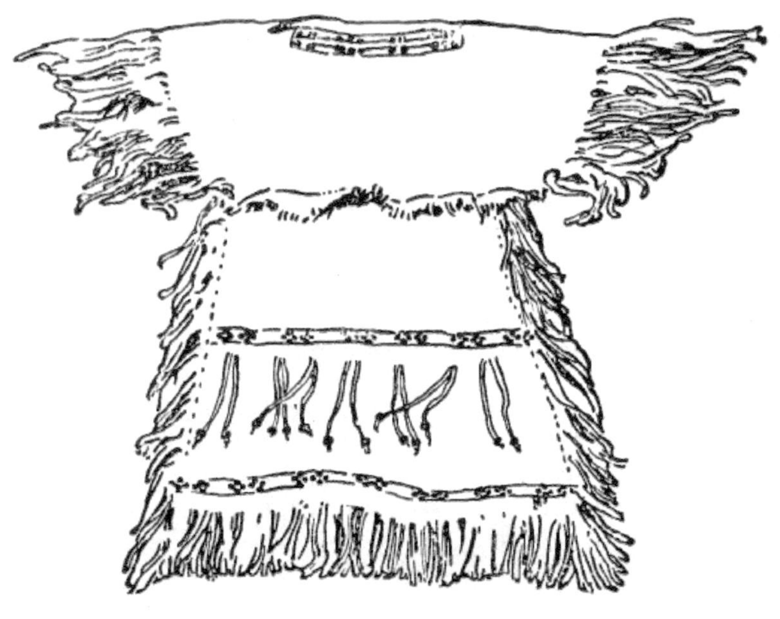

Fig. 44

Although this shirt and the moccasins and leggings that go with it are so simple to make, you are almost sure to need the help of your mother or governess in planning and cutting them. The shirt is the size for a child of seven or eight, but it can easily be enlarged so as to fit a boy of twelve or fourteen. It is made by the pattern shown in Fig. 44, which is drawn on the scale of one inch to a foot. One large chamois skin and two of medium size will be needed. Double the large skin lengthwise to cut the upper part of the shirt. This should be ten inches deep and a yard wide. Cut at the centre a slit about nine inches long for the neck. The ends form the sleeves. Lay the two smaller skins together and cut from them the lower portion of the shirt. The back and front are alike, each measuring nineteen inches wide at the top, twenty-two inches at the bottom, and fifteen inches deep. Make a pencil mark at the centre of each lower edge of the upper part and one at the middle of the top of both of the lower pieces. Turn up an inch at each lower edge of the upper part of the shirt and baste the doubled edge of one side against the top of one of the lower parts, keeping the pencil marks at the middle of each together. Sew the edges together over and over with No. 90 white linen thread. Join the other side in the same way. The overlapping edges of the upper part of the shirt should be kept on the right side. Sew the sides of the shirt together with a row of backstitching, four inches from the edge. The edges are cut into a fringe four and a half inches deep at the ends of the sleeves and three inches on the sides and bottom of the shirt. The edges of the upper part which hangs over the lower are also cut into a short fringe. Work two narrow bands of bead embroidery round the neck, and if you like you can also work a band half way down the lower part of the shirt and one near the lower edge just above the fringe. They are made in this way: Thread a No. 11 needle with white linen thread and make a knot at the other end. Start at the right of the neck close to the edge. Bring the needle through to the outside of the shirt. String four beads, press them down close to the shirt and bring the needle through to the inside. This makes a stitch which runs up and down at right angles with the neck opening. Bring the needle out again on a line with the place where it went in and close beside it, string four more beads, bring it up and run it in again just at the left of where the work began (see Fig. 45). This simple stitch is the one that is most used by the Indians in embroidering their buckskin shirts, leggings and moccasins. String different colours, according to the pattern. Several designs for this work are shown in Figs. 46, 47 and 48. If you wish to decorate the shirt still more, cut strips of chamois about a quarter of an inch wide and five inches long, pierce a row of holes, two together, at intervals of an inch and three-quarters across the shirt (see Fig. 44), bring the strips of chamois through them and tie them once. String a large Indian-red bead on each end and tie a knot to keep it from falling off.

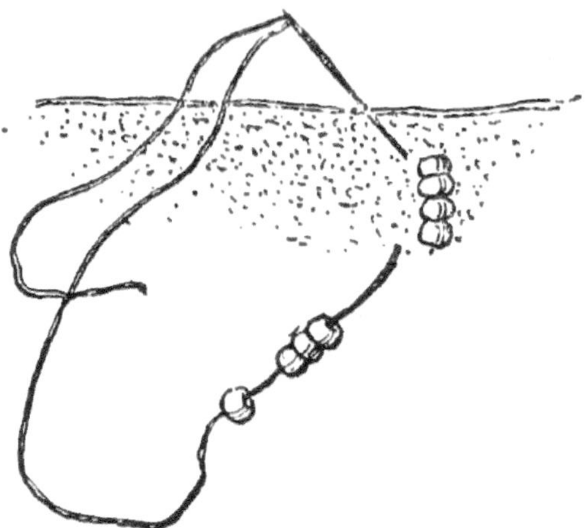

Fig. 45

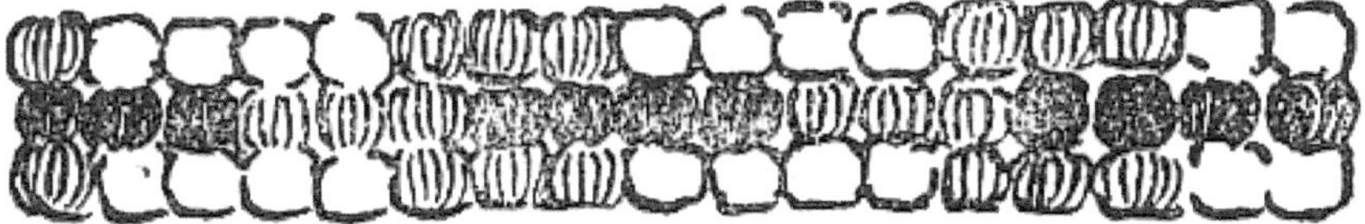

Fig. 46

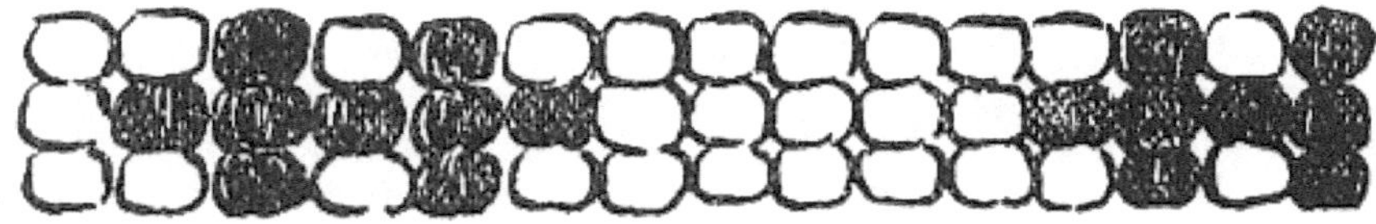

Fig. 47

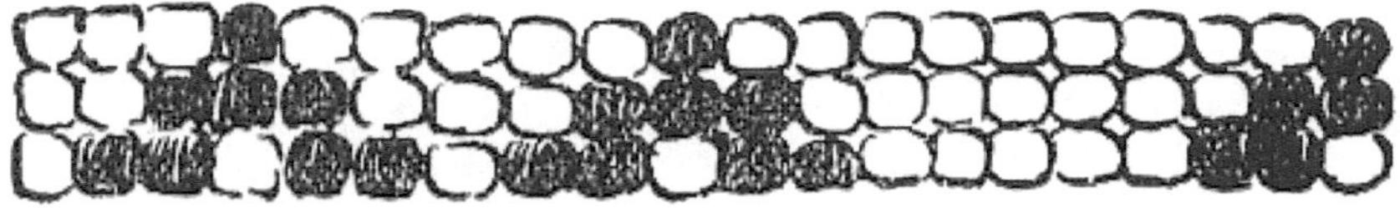

Fig. 48

Indian Leggings

Materials Required: 2 small chamois skins,
½ bunch dark blue beads, No. 4-0,
½ bunch Indian red beads, No. 4-0,
½ bunch white opaque beads, No. 4-0,
A spool of No. 90 white linen thread,
A No. 11 needle.

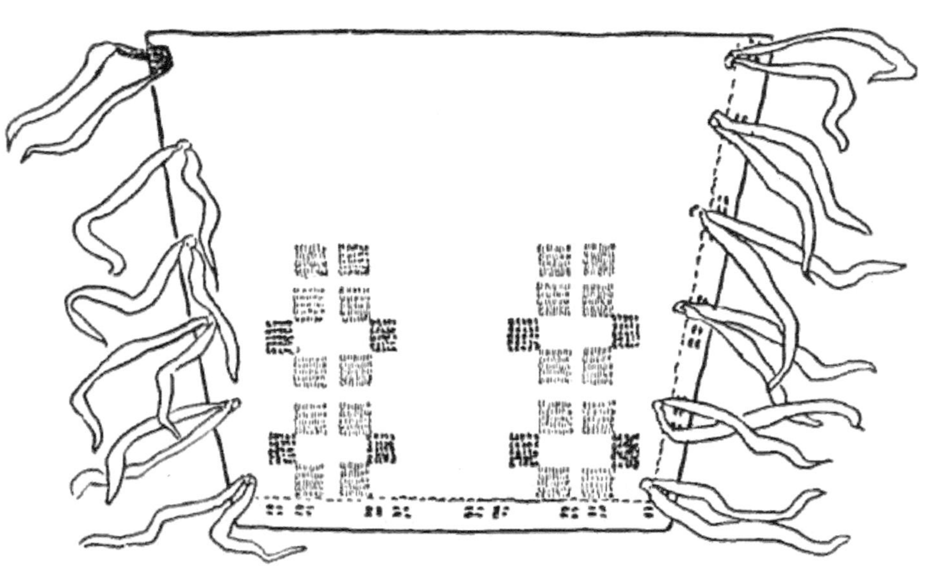

Fig. 49

Fig. 50

Nothing could be easier to make than Indian leggings, and you can put as much work or as little as you choose into the embroidery. Cut from two small chamois skins two pieces in the shape shown in Fig. 49. They should each be eight and three-quarters inches at the lower edge, twelve inches at the top and twelve high. The design shown in Fig. 50 will be simple and effective, and narrow bands like those in Fig. 51 may be worked along the edge that laps over and across the bottom. Six strands of chamois about eight inches long are brought through the leggings on each side at an inch from the edge. These form the fastenings.

Fig. 51

Beaded Moccasins

Materials Required:　　1 medium-sized chamois skin,

½ bunch dark blue beads, No. 4-0,

½ bunch Indian red beads, No. 4-0,

½ bunch white opaque beads, No. 4-0,

1 spool No. 25 white linen thread,

A No. 3 needle,

1 spool No. 90 white linen thread,

A No. 11 needle.

To make the pattern for these moccasins you need only stand on a sheet of brown paper and draw with a pencil around your bare foot so as to get its exact size and natural form. Cut the pattern out and take it to a shoemaker, who will cut from it a pair of leather soles. The uppers you can cut from a paper pattern copied from the shape shown in Fig. 52. It will not be difficult to plan them to fit the soles, for you have only to measure the distance around the outer edge of the soles and make the uppers measure about an inch more along the outer edge, to allow for the seam at the back and for a little fulness across the toe. Work them in some simple design, like the one shown in Fig. 53. A pretty beaded edge is made with a stitch which is very like the one used in working the bands. Thread a needle with No. 90 white linen thread and bring it through the top of the moccasin close to the edge. Fasten the end by taking two or three small stitches. String six beads of a colour used in working the bands and bring the needle through the edge from the inside of the moccasin out, about a quarter of an inch from the beginning, making the stitch shown in Fig. 54. Before starting the next stitch pass the needle under the first one. Work the whole upper edge of the moccasin in this way, then stitch it together up the back, making a seam a quarter of an inch wide. It should be stitched on the inside and then turned right side out. The uppers are stitched on to the soles with a No. 3 needle and a well-waxed piece of white linen thread, No. 25. Should this prove too hard work for small fingers the moccasins may be taken to a shoemaker to finish.

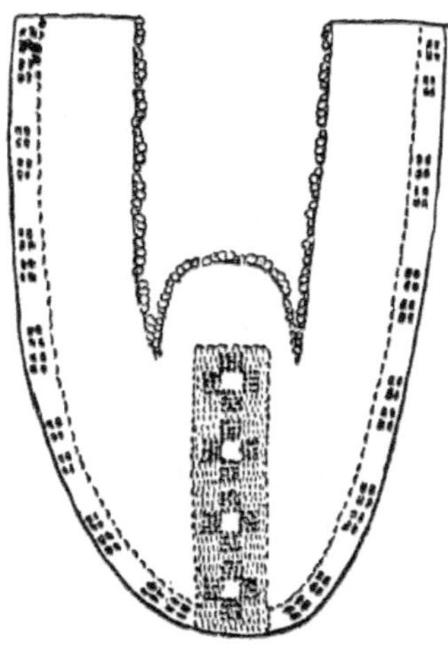

Fig. 52

Fig. 53

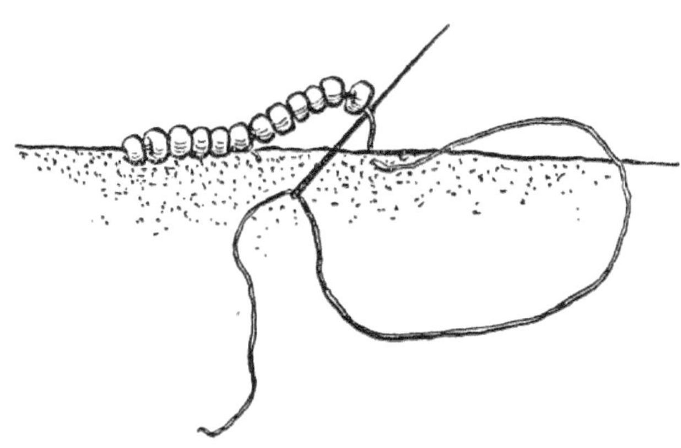

Fig. 54

Bead Wrought Silk Bag

Materials Required: A piece of silk or ribbon, 5 inches wide by 7¾ inches long,

1 bunch of crystal beads, No. 4-0, the same colour as the silk,

1 skein of No. 4-0 beads of a contrasting colour,

A spool of letter A sewing silk of the same colour as the silk,

A No. 11 needle,

A yard of inch-wide ribbon the colour of the silk.

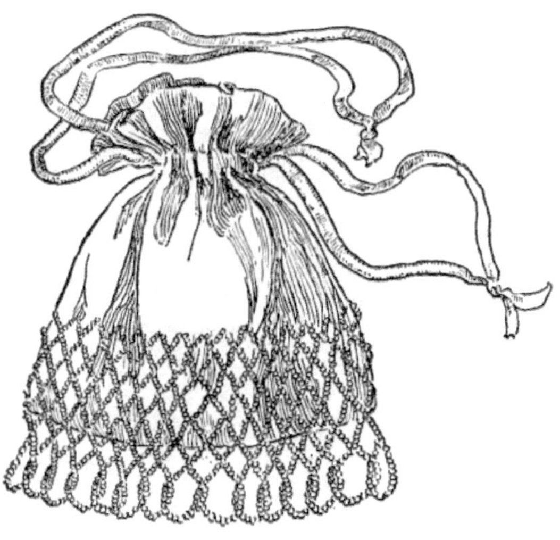

Fig. 55

The daintiest little silk bag may be made by any small daughter for mamma or a dearly-loved aunt to carry a bit of lace work or some other treasure. A piece of soft ribbon five inches wide and seven and three-quarters inches long in a pale shade of lavender makes a charming bag. A network of lavender crystal beads of the same shade, with a pearl or gold-lined crystal bead at the point of each diamond-shaped mesh, gives the finishing touch of daintiness (see Fig. 55). Start by threading a fine needle with a piece of sewing silk the colour of the bag. Fasten the end by taking one or two small stitches near the left side of the strip of silk at about two inches from the lower edge. String six lavender beads, one pearl and seven lavender beads, and take a stitch a quarter of an inch from the beginning and on a line with it. Now run the needle down through the last bead strung (see Fig. 56), and string six more lavender beads, one pearl and seven lavender. Another stitch is made a quarter of an inch from the last one, the needle is run down through the last bead, and it goes on in this way until a row has been made across the piece of silk. The bag is then stitched up the sides and around the bottom on the wrong side and turned right side out. Bring the needle attached to the beadwork down through the six lavender beads and one pearl one, at the left side of the first half diamond made, and string six lavender, one pearl and six lavender beads. Pass the needle through the next pearl bead on the right in the row above and string another six lavender, one pearl and six lavender beads to make another half diamond. So it goes on around the bag. This row and all the other ones are only attached to the row above, not to the silk. The last row of netting should reach a little below the bottom of the bag. A twisted fringe is then made as follows: Run the needle down through the beads on the left side of the first mesh in the row just finished, through the pearl bead at the point, and also pass it through the pearl bead on the back of the bag which lies just beneath it. String thirty lavender beads and pass the needle up through the beads on the right side of the first mesh and down again through those on the left side of the second mesh. It runs through the pearl bead at the point of the mesh and the one under it at the back of the bag. String thirty more beads and twist the thread on which they are strung once around the right side of the loop just made. The next loop is made in the same way—passing the needle up through the beads in the right side of the second mesh, down through those in the left side of the third one, and through the pearl bead at the point of the mesh at the front and the one below it at the back. Thirty more beads are then strung. When you have made this fringe all across the bottom of the bag, fasten the end of the silk by sewing it two or three times through the bottom of the bag. Finish the top of the bag with drawing strings as follows: Turn in a hem three-quarters of an inch wide at the top of the bag and baste it. Hem it around neatly with the lavender sewing silk and make a casing for the drawing strings to run through, by putting a row of backstitching a little over a quarter of an inch above the bottom of the hem. There should be two little holes made on each side of the bag on the outside of the hem between the stitched seam and the bottom of the hem. They are put there so that the ribbon drawing strings can run into the casing. You can make them with an ivory or metal piercer called a stiletto, or any other tool that has a sharp round point. The neatest way to finish these holes is to sew the edges over and over with a needleful of sewing silk. Half a yard of narrow ribbon should be allowed for each drawing string. Thread it in a bodkin, or ribbon needle, which is run into one of the holes at the side of the bag, through the casing at the lower part of the hem, all around the bag and out of the hole beside the one where it went in. Now tie the ends of this drawing string together, thread the other one through the bodkin and run it into a hole on the opposite side of the bag, through the casing all around the bag and out of the little hole beside the one where it went in. The ends of this piece are also tied, and then the bag is done.

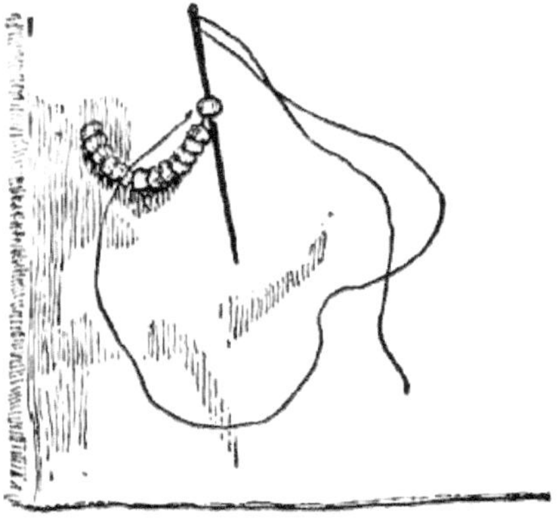

Fig. 56

CHAPTER VI

CLAY WORKING

Have you ever noticed how, when it rains, one road will dry at once, and on another your footprints will hold the water like a cup for hours? Do you know the reason for it? The first road is sandy, and so the water filters through the coarse particles and soon disappears. The other is mostly of clay, which is close and fine, and after your foot made that little hollow it was doubtless half baked by the sun so that it became like natural pottery. You probably know all this, and have felt with your own fingers the difference between the sand, in which you have built forts and dug with your shovel in the summer and played with on the kindergarten sand table in winter, and the soft, smooth clay that you have formed into bird's nests, eggs and other things in kindergarten.

Years and years ago, before our great-great-great-grandfathers were even thought of, some man noticed the same thing that you do—that one part of the earth held water for hours, while it disappeared so quickly from other parts—and it set him thinking. Why not make a bowl in which he could carry water when he was travelling or hunting in dry places? This is the way, some wise men think, the making of pottery began. Cups and small vessels could easily be moulded from small lumps of clay, but large pieces—great bowls and jars—it was soon found would have to be formed in a mould. Shallow baskets, pieces of gourd or fruit rind, were the moulds in which these large pots were started.

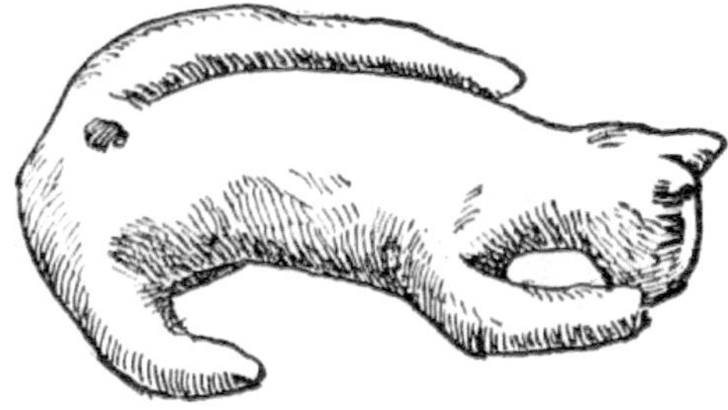

Fig. 57

In beginning the bottom, either a small piece of clay was patted flat into a form like a cookie and fitted into the bottom of the mould, or else a strip of clay was coiled round and round into a mat shape, working the coils together with the fingers. The sides were almost always built up with coils of clay, then, with the fingers and some rude tools—smooth stones, bits of shell or pieces of gourd—they were smoothed and polished. Soon the potters began to decorate their vessels with patterns cut or pressed into the damp clay and even painted them with coloured clay, ground fine and mixed with a liquid. The clay objects you enjoyed making in kindergarten were not very strong. A bowl or cup that is moulded from such clay will not hold water for very long either. It will soon soften and fall to pieces. That is what happened to the first clay bowls and cups.

If clay is baked in the sun it becomes a little harder and more useful—but not much—so the first clay workers found that they must bake their clay pots more thoroughly if they were to be really strong. Some of the old potters—like the Catawba Indians—baked their vessels before the fire, and as the clay they used was very good they found it made them hard enough. In other tribes the potters made a bed of bark, set fire to it and baked the pot until when it came out it was red hot. At first the clay workers used the clay just as they found it, but when they began to make large pots and cauldrons to cook in they found that powdered shell or sand mixed with the clay made them stronger and less liable to crack in baking.

The cooking vessels had almost always rounded bottoms, because in those days the floors of houses were of sand or soft earth into which the rounded bottoms would set and hold the pots upright. These pots were set directly over the fire and kept in position by stones or sticks of wood. Some that had handles or flaring rims could be hung over the fire by cords or vines.

Fig. 58

The Indians moulded all sorts of things out of clay besides these utensils. Drums were made by stretching buckskin over the tops of earthen pots. Then there were whistles and rattles, trowels, modelling tools, figures of men and animals, and many toys like those shown in Figs. 57, 58 and 59. Beads were also made of clay, and so were tobacco pipes in many shapes. One would have the face of a man on the bowl, another a goat with open mouth, or a bird with its neck outstretched and bill parted, and on another the bowl would be formed by a natural-looking snake coiled up for a spring.

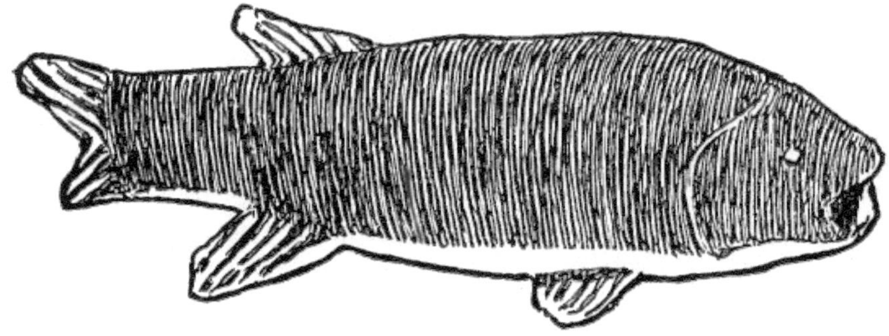

Fig. 59

In time men learned more about clays and how to mix and form and bake them, until now, as you know, pottery that is beautiful and serviceable is made all over the world, and in great factories china and porcelain made of the finest clays are moulded, decorated and fired for our use. It will be interesting to you sometime to see one of the factories where such ware is made, but although it is so fine and smooth and perfect and so useful to us, I doubt if the workmen who make it have half the pleasure in their task that the first potters had in moulding their rough cooking utensils and clay pipes. So I am glad to think that although you may never be able to make china, you can work in clay as the Indians used to do, for that you will enjoy far more.

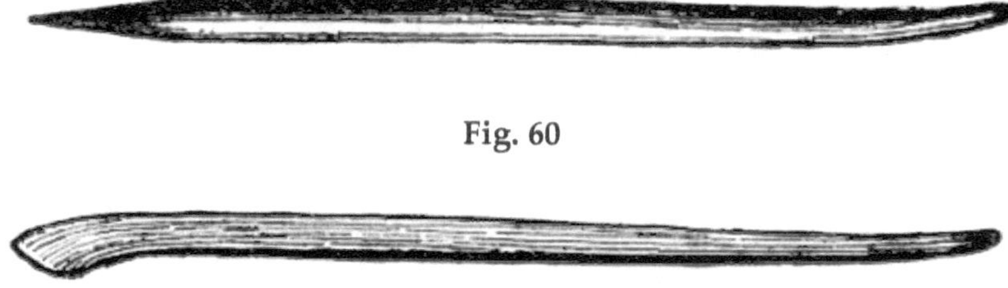

Fig. 60

Fig. 61

Of course you would like to make something that you can use, something that will not crumble and break like the things you modelled in kindergarten. To do this you will need to get a clay which can be baked—or fired, as potters express it—and you must have a clay that is so mixed or arranged as to bake well in the kiln (or pottery oven) to which you are going to send it. If you live near a pottery where flower pots or gray stoneware are made you can probably arrange to buy your clay there, and after your pottery is finished have it baked at the same place. The clay that is used at a stoneware pottery is arranged so as to fire at a much greater heat than the flower-pot clay, and so the ware is stronger, but the flower-pot ware will be strong enough for the things you will make. Although this clay is gray before it is baked, it comes from the kiln a beautiful Indian red.

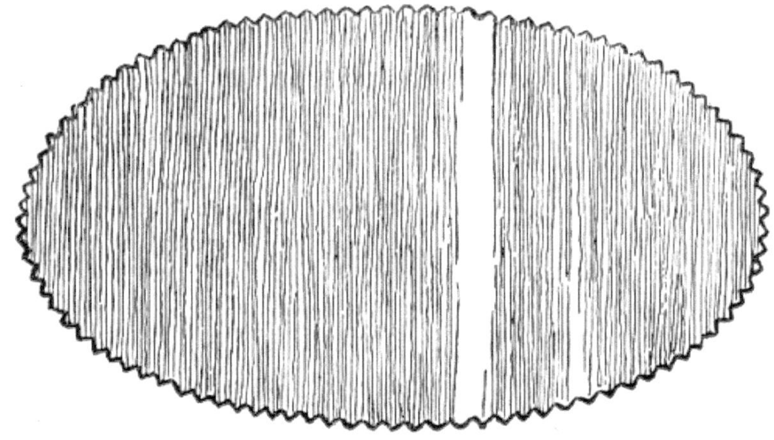

Fig. 62

You will not need many tools beside your own fingers and thumbs. One box-wood modelling tool the shape shown in Fig. 60, and another with more flattened and rounded ends (see Fig. 61) will be enough to begin with. These you can buy at a kindergarten-supply store. Later you may need the sheet-steel tools shown in Figs. 62 and 63. Dealers in hardware sell the sheet steel, and these tools can easily be cut from it—doubtless the dealer will do it for you.

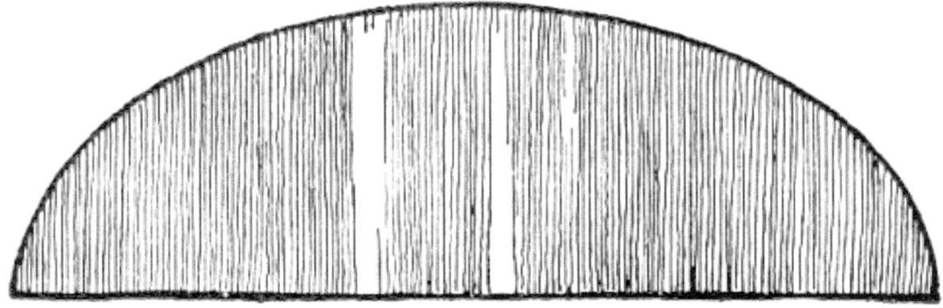

Fig. 63

Buy fifteen or twenty pounds of clay at a time, ready mixed if possible. If it comes to you in the dry state—in rock-like pieces—you must first pound it to a powder. This you can do out of doors by spreading the lumps of clay on a paper laid on flat stone and pounding them with a smaller stone, or, if it must be done in the house, spread the clay on a strong bench or table and pound it with an old flatiron. It is now ready for soaking. Put a little water in an earthen crock and add the powdered clay to it, mixing it with your hand and adding clay until it is the right consistency to mould. If you find you have too much water, pour off some after the clay is well mixed, and if it is still too moist, spread it on a board in the air until it has dried out sufficiently.

Keep the clay in an earthen crock with a cover. Pour a little water into it first, just enough to moisten the bottom of the crock, and then put in the clay. When it is to be left over night or a longer time, make deep holes in the clay with your thumb and pour water into them. Lay a damp cloth over it and cover with the earthen top. If at any time it dries out so that it cannot be easily moulded, let it dry entirely, pound it to powder again and mix as already described.

If you live in the country the place to work with clay will be in an outbuilding, a woodshed, barn or workshop where there is a good strong table or bench. The best place for a city child to work is a playroom where there is a wooden floor, an old table and nothing valuable to be harmed with clay or water; or a light, dry cellar. A girl should wear a long-sleeved apron and a boy a pair of overalls. In such a workshop and costume you need not give a thought to clothes or carpets.

Have a pitcher of water and a small bowl for the "slip"—or clay thinned with water until it is about as thick as cream—which is almost as important as the clay itself.

When you are ready to begin work, take a lump of clay about as large as a grape fruit; pound and knead it on the table. Next draw a strong wire through it, dividing it into halves. Press the two outer surfaces together and knead out the air-holes which you will see on the inner surfaces. Repeat this process several times, and all these air bubbles will finally be expelled. Suppose you begin with something simple—some tiny red building bricks which will delight your small brother—perhaps even you may not feel to old to enjoy playing with such a "real" toy.

Building Bricks

Materials Required: About 3 pounds of clay,

2 level boards, 15 by 20 inches,

½ yard of white cheesecloth,

A rolling pin,

A foot rule,

A strong, sharp knife.

The clay of which these bricks are made should be well kneaded, and it should also have a great deal of what potters call "grog" mixed through it. "Grog" is baked clay pounded into small pieces—an old flower pot will do if you are using flower-pot clay. Mixed with the unbaked clay it tempers it, that is, it makes it less likely to shrink and crack in baking.

Cover a level board with a piece of wet white cheesecloth and tack it securely upon it. Mould the lump of clay into a square, by hand, lay it on the board and pound it with the thick part of your hand into an irregular square cake, then roll it with a rolling pin till it is about three-eighths of an inch thick. Have ready another board the same size and covered with wet cheesecloth, lay it on top of the clay sheet and reverse it so that the clay shall be transferred to this second board. Roll it again till quite smooth and set it away overnight. The next day take a foot rule and a sharp pencil and mark the clay sheet into bricks, two inches long by an inch wide. Cut them out with a strong, sharp knife, but do not lift them until they are thoroughly dry, which will be in three or four days. They should then be carefully packed and sent to the pottery to be fired.

A Clay Whistle

Materials Required: A piece of clay about the size of a lemon,

The wooden modelling tools,

A bowl of slip,

A pen knife.

Fig. 64

The Mexicans mould tiny whistles of clay, which are as simple as possible to make and very fascinating to own. If you would like to make some for yourself and your friends this is the way to do it: Mould a small piece of clay into a cup shape about an inch across and three-eighths of an inch high. Put it in the air to dry for ten minutes. Now roll a piece of clay, about the same size, on the table with the palms of both hands (near the base of the thumb), lightly, yet so as to make the clay roll entirely around with each push. If the roll flattens from too hard pressure, pat it till it is round again and roll it until it is of even thickness—about quarter of an inch in diameter. It is then flattened evenly by patting it with the fingers, one end is cut into a long point and the coil is started on edge with the narrow side up on the top of the cup of clay, whose rim must first be wet with slip. Bend the upper edge of the roll of clay in quite a little, to follow the shape shown in Fig. 64. Hold the long end of the clay strip with the left hand, while, with the thumb and middle finger of the right hand held on each side of the coil to support it, the forefinger presses it down firmly on the top of the little cup. When the coil has gone all the way around cut the end into a flat point, which will fit evenly in with the one at the beginning, and press the edges together with the flat part of the nail of your forefinger. Do this where the edges of the coil come against the rim of the cup. Make quick and firm yet short strokes of the nail up and down, inside the cup and out. Then let it dry for a short time, about ten or fifteen minutes. Roll another coil in the same way and attach it, after brushing the top edge of the clay cup with slip, bending the top edge of the coil in very decidedly so as to leave only a small opening at the top. The third coil is made in the same way, but put on so as to make the sides go straight up like the neck of a bottle or vase. One more straight coil completes the neck, and a piece of clay is then put across the top, closing it. After the whistle has dried for an hour or more a triangular hole is cut with a knife in the lower part (see Fig. 65), and a slit in the top. A hole is also made in the bottom. It should then be thoroughly dried for several days before sending it to be fired. Not every one of these whistles makes a good clear sound, but they are so easy to mould that you will not mind one or two unsuccessful attempts when you finally make one that blows clear and shrill.

Fig. 65

Clay Rattle

Materials Required: A piece of clay about the size of an orange,

A bowl of slip,

The modelling tools.

The Indians used to make clay rattles like the one shown in Fig. 66. It is formed like the whistle except that the cup-shaped piece which is made in starting should be an inch and three-quarters across and three-eighths of an inch high.

Roll the strips of clay as already described and brush the edge of the cup-shaped piece with slip before attaching each coil. The handle should be about three inches long. Before closing the end of it drop in four or five clay pellets, about the size of small peas, which have been well dried in the sun. Then seal it with a piece of clay, let it dry for several days and send it to the pottery to be fired.

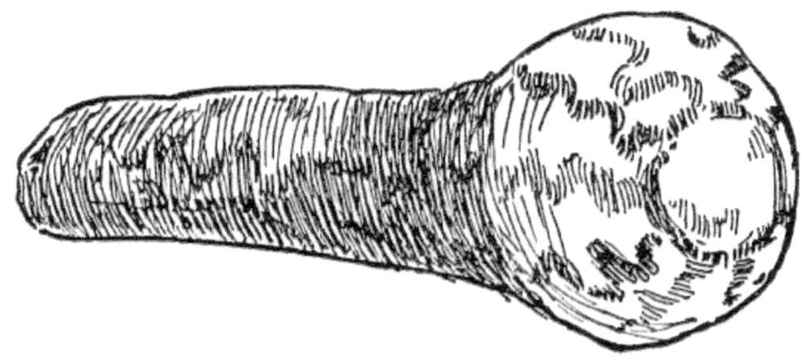

Fig. 66

Birds' Drinking Dish

Materials Required: About 2 ½ pounds of clay,

The wooden modelling tools,

The oval tools of sheet steel,

A bowl of slip,

A low wide bowl,

A small sponge,

A knife,

A ground glass slab about a foot square,

A cloth in which some ground flint is tied.

One of the best ways to attract the birds is to have a drinking dish, wide and generous, always ready for them on the lawn. This is of course taking for granted that you live at least a part of the year in the country. Isn't it delightful to think that you can make such a dish with your own hands? It is a little more difficult than the other things you have made, but what of that—it will be worth the trouble if you can give a lawn party to the birds every day! As this is to be quite a large dish, you will need to have a mould to form it in, or at least to support the sides in starting. Choose some low, wide bowl or dish, one about two inches high and ten inches across the top. Have ready some powdered flint tied up in a piece of cotton cloth—you can buy it of dealers in potters' supplies or possibly at the pottery where your clay work is fired. This is to dust over the inside of the mould to prevent the clay from sticking to it. Take a lump of clay, about two and a half pounds, knead and pound it until all the air bubbles are worked out. A small piece of the clay is then patted out with the hands on a table or board and rolled smooth with a rolling pin until it is three-eighths of an inch thick and about two inches wider than the bottom of the bowl you have chosen. Lay it in the bottom of the mould, which has first been dusted with ground flint. Press the clay lightly but carefully against the bottom and sides, making sure that it fits close against them. Then cut the top edge even with one of the wooden modelling tools. With the same tool cut crisscross strokes in this upper edge and wet it with slip, to prepare it for the first coil of clay, which is made and attached like those used in forming the whistle. These coils should, however, be larger—about an inch wide and long enough to go all around the bowl once. Join every coil in the same way, taking care to press each one against the sides of the mould as well as upon the coil beneath, and to smooth the inside of the bowl with your fingers and the modelling tools. After attaching a coil, let the bowl dry for ten or fifteen minutes—in the air, unless it is a cold day. Be careful never to let your clay work freeze or it will be spoiled. When the bowl is about two inches and a half high set it away overnight to dry. In the morning it will have shrunk so that it will slip easily out of the mould. Turn it bottom up on a table and wet the cracks between the coils with slip, then fill them in carefully with clay of the same stiffness as that of which the bowl is made. Never put water or wet clay on a piece of clay work that is almost dry, or it will crack. After it has been set away for a few hours to harden, make it smooth and even as follows: First take the oval tool of sheet steel with rough edges, hold it in your right hand, not straight but bent to fit the curves of the outside of the bowl; with it scrape the large humps away from the sides of the bowl, making quick, light and short strokes in every direction—up, down, across and diagonally. When the largest humps have been removed, go over the bowl in the same way with the smooth-edged oval tool. Then take a damp sponge, one from which the water has all been squeezed, and pass it lightly over the bowl, smoothing it with the fingers. Make it as even and perfect as you can.

Next the bottom is to be finished. Draw with a pencil a circle on the bottom of the bowl, about an inch in from the edge all around, and scrape, with the sharpest wooden tool, a layer of clay out of the bottom within the circle, so that the outside ring shall form a ridge about one-sixteenth of an inch above it. Now cut the top edge of the bowl as even as you can by eye, using a knife. Then make it perfectly even in this way: Pour a little water on the ground-glass slab, hold the bowl bottom up and move it firmly yet quickly round and round on the wet surface and then quickly slide it off at the edge of the slab, before it has a chance to cling to the glass. If the bowl seems too heavy for you to hold securely in moving it about so quickly, it will be wise to let an older person do this for you. Then there will be nothing more to do but let it dry for a few days and send it to the pottery to be fired.

CHAPTER VII

INDOOR GARDENING

A Rainy Day in October

All summer long the out-of-door gardens kept us busy, planting, weeding and watering. When we had had a week or two of sunshiny weather we began to wish a cloud would sail over the blue sky and bring the rain our thirsty flowers needed. We could see the reason for rainy days in summer-time. Now, however, it is different; a rainy day in autumn is so cold and disagreeable. It settles down to work in a business-like way—not like a summer shower, which has, all through, a hint of the sun behind the clouds. No, an autumn rain is chilly and gray and lasting, and the best way to forget it is to find something interesting to do indoors.

Suppose we plan an indoor garden. There are the plants that were brought in from the garden the other day—geraniums, heliotropes, lobelias and begonias— all need our care and attention. A boy with a taste for woodworking can make a shelf and put up brackets in a window where the sun will reach them. Even a plant table may not prove too difficult for him.

There is one particularly interesting thing that both boys and girls can do, and that is to plan Christmas gifts of budded or blossoming plants for their family and friends. How is it to be done? Why, by planting bulbs in October. You have seen bulbs, of course, at the florists; they are mostly dingy brown or yellow and look like onions. If anyone in the family had a garden last summer there will be sure to be catalogues of seeds and bulbs in the house, and you can begin by making a list of the bulbs you wish to send for. Such a number as you have to choose from—tulips, crocuses, lilies, hyacinths, narcissus, daffodils, and plenty more. They are not costly either. Hyacinths can be bought for from six to fifteen cents each; these are the ordinary ones. Roman hyacinths, which have beautiful white flowers, cost only four or five cents. Chinese lily bulbs are more expensive; one can be bought for ten cents or three for twenty-five cents, but they are large and the blossoms are so fragrant and beautiful that they are well worth it. These are grown among pebbles in a dish of water. They will look well in a glass dish or in a shallow pottery bowl— such as you can buy for ten or fifteen cents at a Japanese store. For hyacinths, tall, slender glasses are to be had at the florist's for fifteen cents. They come in several colours, but the dark green is best—and that reminds me that there is a case you can make of rattan and raffia around one of these glasses to enable you to hang it beside a window. This you can do some other rainy day.

The Chinese lily bulbs are put into a dishful of tepid water which has a few small pieces of charcoal in it. A number of small stones are fitted around the bulbs to keep them upright and steady, and then they are put near a window where the sun comes. Hyacinths may be grown in the glasses or in flower pots, just as one chooses. A mixture of good soil from the garden and sand is best if they are to be grown in pots. Be careful in taking the garden soil to sift it through your fingers, making sure that no worms are lurking in it, to trouble the bulbs later on. Put stones for drainage and some pieces of charcoal at the bottom of each pot. The bulb is planted so that about one-third of it is left above the earth. If it is to be grown in water, use rain water and fill the glass so that the base of the bulb will just touch it. However they are planted, in pots or in glasses, they should be left in a dark, cool place like an airy cellar, until they are rooted. This will take about two weeks for those in glasses and six for the potted hyacinths. If it is possible, bury the pots in the open ground about six inches deep, or cover them with soil, for about five weeks. They can then be put into the window garden. Consult the bulb catalogues for suggestions as to the care of your plants.

Basket Case for a Hyacinth Glass

Materials Required: A dark green hyacinth glass,

2 weavers of No. 2 rattan,

2 weavers of No. 2 black rattan,

A bunch of copper red raffia,

A tapestry needle, No. 19.

After you have bought your hyacinth glasses, and before the bulbs are put into them, you may like to make for each a simple case of basket work by which it can be hung against the window frame.

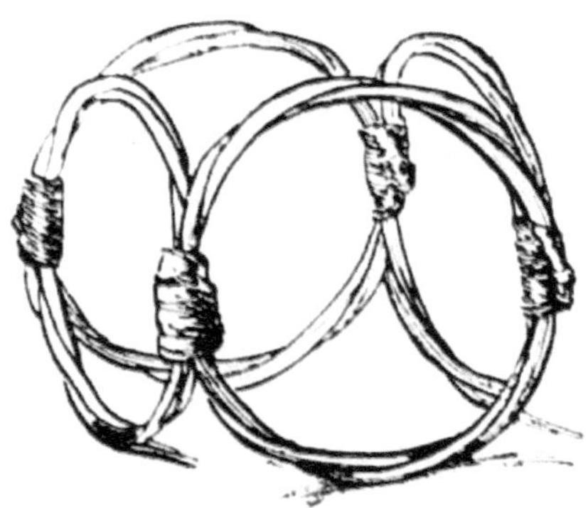

Fig. 67

It is made of rattan rings bound together with raffia of some colour that will look well with the hyacinth blossoms. A dark green glass with a covering of black and the natural-coloured rattan bound with copper-coloured raffia is a good combination, if the hyacinth is to be white.

Make two rings of black rattan like those described in the directions for making a sponge bag (see Chapter IV). One should be large enough to slip over the glass, down to about half an inch from the bottom of it, the other to three inches from the bottom. This second ring must be made on the glass, as the flaring top will not allow so small a ring to slip over it. This will not be difficult to do. Tie the rattan around the glass just below where you wish it to be placed (about two and three-quarters inches from the bottom), then slip it up where the glass is narrower and twist the ends around this foundation ring twice, as shown in Fig. 22. This makes a ring of three circuits, the foundation ring counting as one. Make four rings of the natural-coloured rattan, each measuring two inches and a quarter in diameter on the inside. These are made with two circuits; that is, after tying the foundation ring the ends are twisted all the way around it once, instead of twice as the black ones were, and are cut just so that they will lap. Bind these four rings together in a hollow square with bindings five-eighths of an inch long of raffia in buttonhole stitch (see Fig. 67). Fasten the ends of the rings by making the binding come over them. Slip this square over the top of the glass and down between the two black rattan rings. Here each of the four light rings is bound with raffia in buttonhole stitch to the black ring above it, as well as to the one below. To make a loop to hang it by, tie a ring of black rattan around the neck of the glass, twist its ends twice around it, and then without cutting the ends tie them into another ring an inch and a quarter in diameter, inside measurement, which stands out from the glass and forms a loop. This ring is made with two circuits.

Growing Plants in Fibre

Later on, in November and December, there may come days when you are kept indoors, and then perhaps you will like to do some more gardening with bulbs. Shall we begin with the spring bulbs—tulips, crocuses and daffodils? It is wonderful, isn't it, to think of being able to plant them when out of doors the earth is covered thick with snow? This is how it is done: Buy from a florist or seedsman a fibre mixture which they sell for this purpose. Take a large tub or pail and put some fibre into it, add plenty of water and stir the fibre thoroughly with a stick. Let it remain in the water for two days, stirring it from time to time so that it shall get water soaked. It will then be ready for use. If you plan to give the plants away when they are in bud they should be started in jars or bowls that can be included in the gift. Japanese or Spanish pottery bowls can be bought for from ten to twenty-five cents each, and one of these with a daffodil or narcissus growing in it will make a delightful birthday gift for someone you love. If you are not planning to give them away, of course you will be able to collect about the house enough bowls and jars of china and pottery to hold them. Put a few pieces of charcoal at the bottom of each dish—these are to keep the water pure and the fibre wet. Put into each bowl some of the wetted fibre until it is about two or three inches deep, depending on the depth of the bowl. Place the bulbs on the fibre so that they just touch and fill all in with the wet fibre. Put more fibre over them and press it gently down and around them—not too hard. Fill the dish in until it is nearly solid. Now put the bowls away in a cellar or any dark but airy room where they will not get frostbitten and watch them day by day to see that the fibre does not get dry; it must be kept moist but not soaking wet. Be especially careful that the bulbs do not get dry. When they are all rooted and have grown perhaps an inch, bring the bulbs into a lighter room and let them have plenty of air. Put them on the window sill or even in the garden in the middle of the day, if it is not too cold, and as they begin to show some buds water regularly and often.

Planting Indoors in February

As early as February you can begin to plan your out-of-door flower garden and start some seeds indoors. Tuberous begonias, Canterbury bells, verbenas, single dahlias, scarlet sage or salvia, tufted pansies and cosmos can all be started now. First of all you will need some flats or low wooden boxes—they should be about three inches deep and not too large to handle. If it is possible to get such shallow boxes at your grocer's so much the better, otherwise you can have a soap box or two sawed down to the required height. If they have no cracks or holes for drainage, bore some and partly cover them with pieces of an old flower pot, rounded side up. Put pebbles or other rough material in the bottom of the box. Now you are ready for the soil. Get good, rich loam from the garden and sift it into the boxes. You can then begin planting. The large seeds should be planted about half an inch deep, medium sized ones as deep as four times their own width; the very small ones are just pressed into the earth, and the smallest should have a piece of glass placed over the box so that they will not dry out entirely. Wet the soil until it is quite moist and press it with a level board after planting. Set the boxes in a sunny window, one that faces south or southeast, and keep them moist, but not wet, with a bulb sprinkler (see Fig. 68).

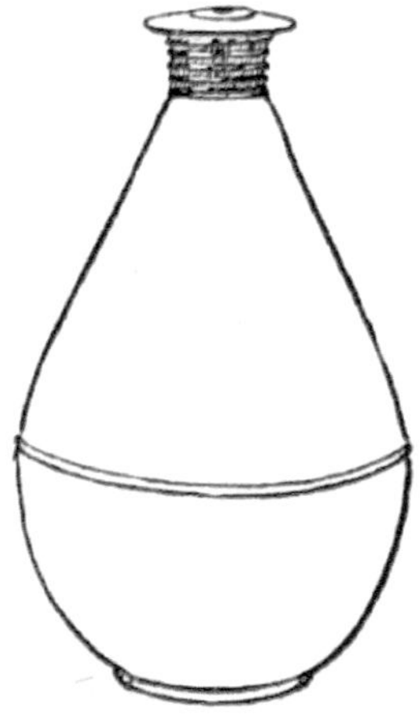

Fig. 68

March Planting

This blustery month of bad weather out of doors you can have a delightful time with your indoor garden. The bulbs you started in fibre should be in bloom by this time, and while you are enjoying them you can start some flower seeds for your out-of-door garden.

A Little Garden for a Little Girl

This is the time to plant what are called annuals—that is, plants that live just a year—like batchelor's-buttons, sweet peas, nasturtiums, four-o'clocks, marigolds and zinnias. Use flats or shallow wooden boxes, like those already described, to plant in. Choose good garden soil and, before filling the boxes, heat it in the oven, very hot—this will kill the weed seeds. Sow the seeds in rows an inch and a half apart and three-quarters of an inch apart in the row. When all the seeds are up, thin the little plants out so that they will be an inch and a half apart in the row. Put them in a sunny window as close to the glass as possible and keep the shades rolled high. If you do not give them enough sun they will become thin and spindly—like children who never go out. Turn the boxes now and then so that all sides will get the sunlight. You will need to put some labels into each box, bearing the names of the seeds that are planted there. The best ones are made from the covers of old grape baskets. Cut them into strips, write on each the name of the seed and the date, and stick it into the earth.

Gradually as the weather gets warmer you can give the little plants more air by opening the windows, and later by putting them out of doors in some sheltered but sunny spot. When there is no longer any danger from frost, the boxes can be set out of doors day and night, only taking them in in case of a severe storm.

The seedlings may need to be separated and transplanted indoors before it is warm enough to set them in the out-of-door garden. Common grape baskets do very well for this purpose and hold about a dozen little plants—flats may also be used. Allow as much space between the seedlings as possible, for if they are too close the roots will twine about each other and make it very hard to transplant them later on. When they are large enough to be transplanted put them into a basin of lukewarm water and plant them in their new box one at a time. Do not put them in the sun for a few days, but keep them shaded until they have taken root.

Starting Gourd Vines in the Indoor Garden

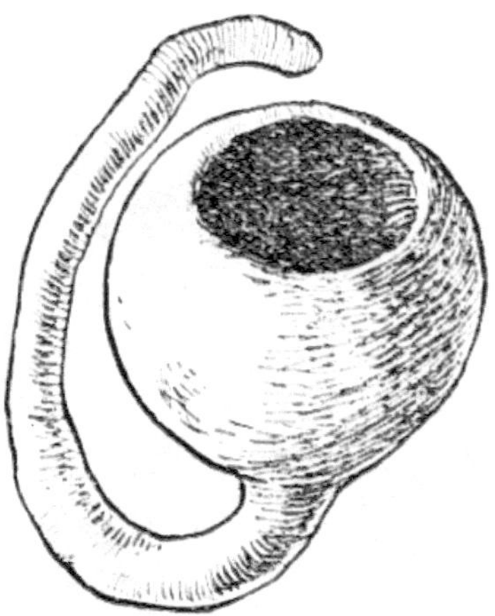

Fig. 69

Of course you have seen gourds, perhaps not growing, but surely you know how they look when dried. Hard, smooth-shelled things of a beautiful golden brown colour, they grow in the strangest shapes. Some are round or oval with a queer twisted stem (see Fig. 69). They have many uses—to hold the stockings open and smooth (so that grandma can darn them easily), as bird houses, match holders, and even for drinking cups.

They are the fruit of a vine which would be charming to train on a trellis or arbour in your out-of-door garden, and then when harvest time came you would have the interesting gourds to dry and use as you chose.

If you would like to raise them, sow the seeds in shallow wooden boxes indoors in March. Plant them a quarter of an inch deep, and when the little plants crowd one another and are strong enough to transplant remove them to larger boxes and plant them six inches apart. When planting the vines out of doors in May or June put plenty of manure about them and give them ample space. If the vines bear many gourds, and all small ones, pinch off some and the others will develop better. Do not pick the gourds until they are quite ripe; that is, when they begin to look slightly yellow. They need plenty of hot sun in order to come to perfection. Leave them as long as possible on the vines, only being careful that they are not touched with frost. In the South they are sometimes left on the vines all winter.

After picking them, hang them in an airy place in the house or out of doors. Leave a little of the vine on each one and they can then be hung by strings tied to these handles. If you follow these few rules your gourds should dry smooth and hard.

How to Start Lavender Indoors

Do you know the smell of lavender—that sweet, refreshing perfume that clings to some of grandmother's treasures of linen and embroidery? One catches a whiff of it in old gardens sometimes, and it is always welcome. You can buy the seed from a florist or seedsman—*Lavandula vera* is what the true English lavender is called, and that is best. If it cannot be had, *Lavandula spica* is next best. It takes time to raise either, but it will be such an addition to your out-of-door garden that you will not regret the time spent. About the first of March the lavender seed should be sown, in window boxes or flats. Make shallow drills with your finger, drop the seed in and cover lightly. Sprinkle them every day with your bulb sprinkler until they come up. When the little plants each have four leaves they may be transplanted. Before starting to transplant them they should be thoroughly wet. Set them five inches apart. In the winter protect the plants with litter—leaves, straw, etc.—six inches deep. The next year, in March, they should be set in rows three feet apart.

When the plants are in full bloom the sprigs are cut, and then dried in a cool, darkened room or closet. Lay them on paper so as to save all the blossoms. The lavender flowers may be made into the daintiest of sachets by filling with them sheer linen bags or pale lavender silk ones.

The sprigs that are left after the blossoms have fallen may be used like Chinese incense to sweeten a room, by lighting the blossom end of a single piece and letting it burn in a vase or incense holder.

CHAPTER VIII

GIFTS AND HOW TO MAKE THEM

It is wonderful what your head and hands can do when you begin to plan gifts for family and friends at Christmas, birthdays and the in-between times when "un-birthday presents" — as "Alice in Wonderland" called them — are so welcome. But I am sure you know the breathless feeling of having to make or buy a long list of Christmas presents with only two weeks or so in which to accomplish it. Why not keep a gift box or drawer, where you can pack away the pretty things you take such pleasure in making on dull days all the year round? There are ever so many things — games, toys, baskets and beadwork — which you will find in other chapters — that will help to fill this gift box, and I am going to tell you about some others.

There are several things to think of in planning a gift. It should be something that will be within your means, something that is worth giving, however small — not "trash"; but what is most important of all is that it shall really please the one who receives it. If it can be a lasting pleasure so much the better.

Suppose you try keeping a notebook; begin it now, and write down the little things that you hear the family wish for during the year — tiny things, maybe, but just what they want. For instance, Aunt Helen, who writes, never has enough pencils — her nieces and nephews know why. Father is unable to find an express tag when he wants one, because he has no case to hang close beside his desk. Joe says he wishes someone would make him a chamois cover for his new knife — it is getting scratched already; and mamma cannot find that recipe for potted pigeons that she cut from the paper Saturday evening. What a number of entries you will be able to make in your gift book! See how it reads:

Aunt Helen: One dozen pencils.

Father: Leather tag case and tags.

Mother: A blank book with her newspaper recipes pasted in.

Joe: A chamois knife case.

And this is just a beginning. When you visit your friends you will soon see or hear what little things will please them. Then you can begin collecting the materials for your gift box, and when a rainy day comes what pleasant hours you will spend.

Let us begin with the

Beaded Knife Case

Materials Required: Some scraps of chamois skin in the natural or another colour,

1 skein No. 4-0 beads in a colour that will harmonise with the leather,

1 E bead of the same colour,

A spool of letter A sewing silk the colour of the leather,

A No. 11 needle.

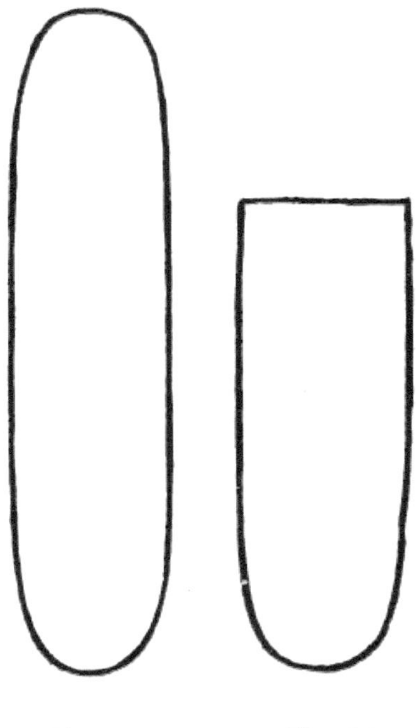

Fig. 70   Fig. 71

One of the simplest and prettiest gifts you can make is this beaded knife case. If you have made the Indian costume described in Chapter V. you will have plenty of scraps of chamois left. Otherwise you can buy a small chamois skin in the natural colour, or, if you prefer another colour, skins of beautiful tints may be bought. Red is very effective and not as costly as some others. In buying a skin, choose a colour that you will not tire of, for you will be able to make so many small things of it that it will be well to have a colour you will always like; either red or green or a soft brown that is not too light will be a good choice.

From a piece of cardboard cut the patterns shown in Figs. 70 and 71. If the case is for a penknife, the larger one (Fig. 70) should measure one inch wide by four and one-eighth inches long, and the other should be the same width but two and three-quarters inches long. Cut two pieces of chamois from these patterns, lay the smaller one against the larger, with the rounded ends of both together and the edges of the sides fitted evenly, and baste them so. Now start at the top left-hand edge of the smaller piece, where it comes against the edge of the larger one, and sew the edges together with the stitch shown in Fig. 72. This is how it is done: Thread a No. 11 needle with sewing silk the colour of the chamois. Fasten the end by sewing through and through the edges of the case. String three beads and make one over-and-over stitch through both edges of the case, bringing the needle out at about one-eighth of an inch from where it started. Run the needle up through the third bead, string two more, make another stitch, run the needle up through the last bead strung, and so on. When you have gone all the way around the double edge, continue the stitch across the top of the smaller piece and around the rounded top of the larger. Next a loop must be made to fasten the case. Hold a small pencil at the top of the larger piece of chamois close to the rounded edge, and, starting about an eighth of an inch from the centre of this end, fasten an end of a needleful of sewing silk; take a stitch around the pencil and in at one-eighth of an inch the other side of the centre. Take six or eight stitches back and forth in this way. This will make a loop, which should be covered with buttonhole stitches. Now slip the knife into the case, turn the flap (the rounded edge of the larger piece) down and mark the place to sew the large bead over which the loop is to fit, in order to fasten it. Sew an E bead the colour of the smaller beads at this place, bring the loop over it, and the case is complete.

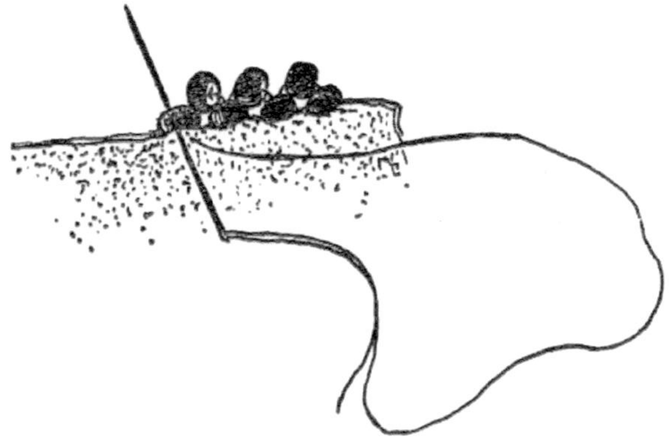

Fig. 72

Needle Book of Flowered Silk

Materials Required: A piece of flowered silk or ribbon 5 inches long by 3 ½ inches wide,

A piece of plain-coloured ribbon the same size,

A piece of white flannel 10 inches long by 7 inches wide,

½ yard of narrow ribbon the colour of the silk,

A spool of sewing silk the same colour,

A piece of bristol board 10 by 7 inches.

The Shakers make needle books of fine straw cloth, that are so dainty and yet simple that they are well worth copying. Fig. 73 shows the shape in which the cover of the book is cut. It may be made of two pieces of bristol board; one covered with flowered silk or ribbon, the other with plain silk that will harmonise with the flowered. The two are then basted together and sewed over and over. Two pieces of flannel are cut the same shape, but about half an inch smaller all the way around. These are laid inside the cover, which is then bent exactly at its centre so that both ends will come evenly together. A hole is punched through both sides of the cover and the flannel at about half an inch in from the edge and quarter of an inch from the doubled middle of the cover. Another hole is made on the other side of it and a narrow ribbon threaded in a bodkin, or ribbon needle, is brought in through one hole, across the back and out through the other. The ends are then tied in a pretty bow (see Fig. 74), which finishes it.

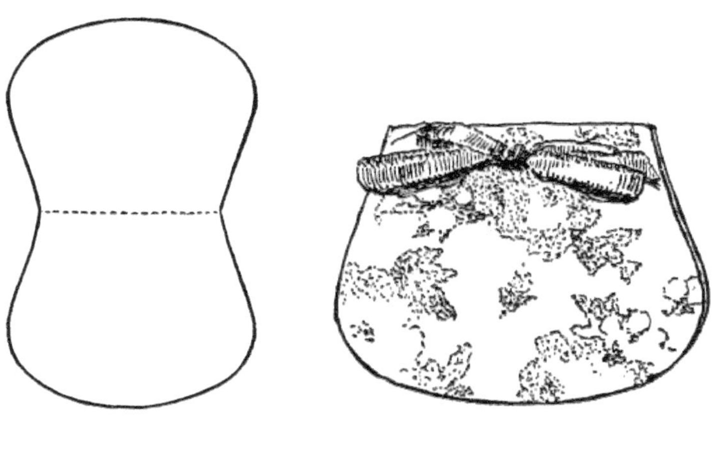

Fig. 73   Fig. 74

Sweet Clover Bags

Materials Required: All the white sweet clover that a little child can gather,

Some pretty cotton cloth,

A needle and thread,

Scissors.

Did you know that the white sweet clover that grows in long spike-shaped sprays on low bushes along the wayside is even more fragrant when it is dried? Gather some this summer, and spread it where it will dry in the sun, turning it often. Strip the blossoms from the stems, and when a rainy day comes you can make with them some gifts that will be welcome wherever they go. Keep the flowers in a covered box till you are ready to use them, then make linen, or even pretty white cotton, bags about ten inches long by six wide. Fill them with the dried clover, sew up the ends securely, and they will be ready to send to grandmothers, aunts and cousins, to make their linen closets fragrant. A little pillow of white cotton filled with these flowers, with a pretty outer case of fine linen, makes a delightful gift for an invalid friend.

Eyeglass Cleaner

Materials Required: Several sheets of soft white tissue paper,

A piece of green or brown leather 4 inches wide by 6 ½ inches long,

A strip of leather 15 inches long by ¼ of an inch wide,

1 skein No. 3-0 beads,

2 large beads of the same colour,

An awl or punch.

One of your friends who wears eyeglasses was told by a wise person that the best thing with which to clear her glasses was—what do you think? Not a handkerchief or a piece of chamois, but soft tissue paper. "That is simple enough, I'm sure," said she; but it wasn't, for whenever she wanted a piece of tissue paper it didn't happen to be near, so she used a handkerchief or chamois most of the time. She found the tissue paper was much better, however, and wondered why children who don't know what to give to friends who wear eyeglasses or spectacles, don't give them a pad of tissue paper to hang by the dressing table or some such convenient place. True, its use would have to be explained, for not many people know that tissue paper is such a good cleaner of glasses; but when they have tried it they will be really grateful for the helpful little gift.

Cut soft white tissue paper in sheets four inches wide by six and one-half long, and make a cover of green or brown leather the same size. Punch two holes at the top of the cover, each about half an inch down from the top and one inch in from the side. Lay the cover on the pile of tissue paper sheets and run an awl or punch through the holes in the cover, making holes in the same places through the tissue paper. Cut a strip of leather about one-quarter of an inch wide and fifteen inches long, thread it in a bodkin, run it through the hole on the right of the cover, through the sheets of tissue paper and out of the hole on the left of the cover. Here it is tied in a bow, leaving a long loop at the back to hang it by. A large bead of a colour that will look well with the leather may be strung on each end of the bow and a knot tied to keep it from falling off. If you choose, the edges of the cover may be worked with the bead stitch shown in Fig. 54.

A German Wonder Ball

Materials Required: 1 hank of single zephyr worsted of some pretty colour,

Several tiny gifts.

One of the most delightful of gifts can be planned by a little girl of boy for a friend who is learning to knit. This is the wonder ball. It is one of the many good ideas that come to us from Germany—the land of knitting.

Buy a hank of worsted of some pretty colour and a number of tiny gifts—a thimble, a wee package of chocolate, the smallest of baskets and any other little things you can think of. Start winding the worsted around the very choicest gift—so that it shall be at the centre—then by degrees, as you wind, lay the other gifts on the ball and cover them with the worsted. Your little friend should be told to knit till all the presents are found.

Pin Case for Travelling

Materials Required: A piece of flowered silk or ribbon 8 inches long by 5 inches wide,

A piece of plain-coloured silk 8 inches long by

5 ½ inches wide,

A piece of cotton wadding 7 ½ inches long by

4 ½ inches wide,

½ yard of ribbon ½-inch wide, the colour of the silk,

A spool of sewing silk the same colour.

The friend who travels will be glad to have a case in which to keep her pins. It is very simple to make.

Cut from any pretty piece of silk or velvet a strip five inches wide by eight long, or a piece of five-inch flowered ribbon the same length will do even better. Another strip of thin silk—white or some colour that will look well with the first piece—should be cut the same size, if the flowered piece is of silk; if it is of ribbon, cut the lining silk half an inch wider. A piece of the cotton wadding that comes in sheets is cut half an inch smaller in length and width than the others. Half a yard of narrow ribbon to match the silk, and a spool of sewing silk will also be needed, and if you like you can give a still more festive touch to the case by filling it with fancy pins, those with pearl or gun-metal heads.

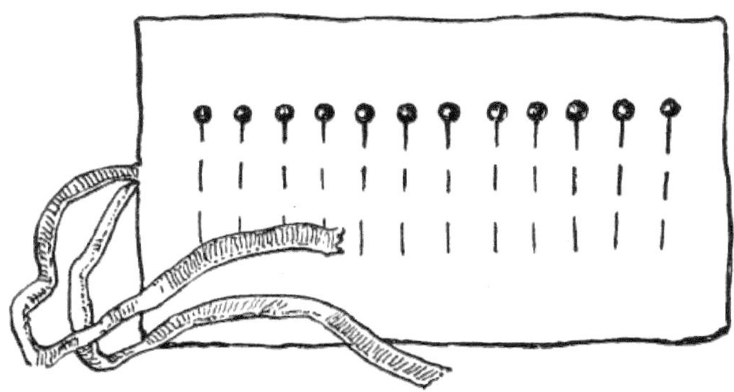

Fig. 75

First baste the strip of cotton wadding on the lining silk through the centre, then turn quarter of an inch of the edge of the silk up over the wadding and baste it securely around all four sides. Now baste the flowered silk cover against the other side of the wadding, turning in all rough edges, and making sure that the edges of the lining and cover are quite even, one above the other. Sew them together over and over, as neatly as possible, with the coloured sewing silk, and stitch the ribbon at its centre to the middle of one end of the case to form strings (see Fig. 75). After it is filled with the pretty pins and rolled up, bring the ribbons around it and tie them in a dainty little bow.

A Case for Tape

Materials Required: A piece of flowered or figured cotton
8 inches long by 4 ½ inches wide,
A piece of plain-coloured cotton the same size,
¾ yard of ½-inch ribbon the colour of the cotton,
A package of India tape,
A bodkin,
A spool of cotton.

A case that is made in very much the same way as the one for pins is used for holding pieces of tape of various widths. It is something that almost any aunt would be delighted to have for her work basket.

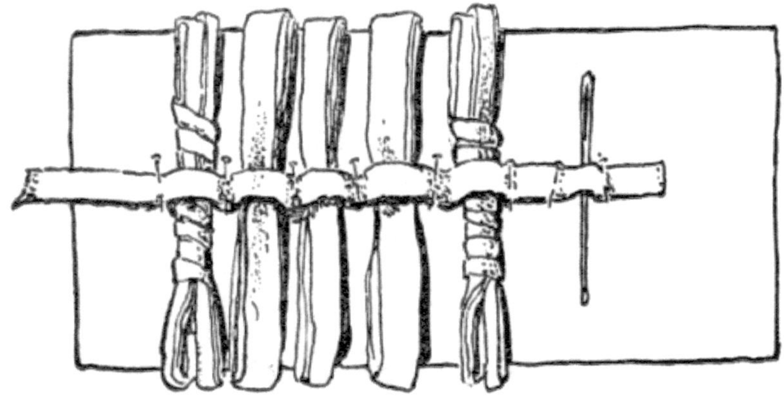

Fig. 76

Packages of what is called India tape are sold at many of the dry goods shops for five or ten cents. They contain bunches of tape of different widths, a yard or two in each bunch. Pieces of pretty cotton, one figured or flowered, the other plain, will do quite as well as silk to make the case. Then you will need a simple metal or bone bodkin and three-quarters of a yard of narrow ribbon or silk braid. That is all except a spool of cotton, needle and scissors.

Cut a piece of plain-coloured cotton eight inches long by four and a half wide, and lay the bunches of tape all along it, about an inch apart. Now lay a piece of half-inch wide ribbon or silk braid along above the bunches of tape and exactly at the middle of the strip of cotton, as shown in Fig. 76. Pin the ribbon to the cotton lining at each side of every piece of tape, making a loop that is large enough for each bunch to slip through without pulling the cotton lining. A little loop should also be made just large enough to hold the bodkin. Now take out the bunches of tape and stitch the ribbon to the lining where it is pinned. Cut a piece of flowered cotton the same size as the lining, and, turning in the edges of both pieces for a quarter of an inch all the way round, lay them together with the raw edges in and baste them evenly one above the other. Next sew them together over and over all around. Stitch the middle of a piece of ribbon sixteen inches long to the middle of the right end of the case, slip the bunches of tape and the bodkin through their loops, roll the case and tie the ribbon strings around it. It will then be ready to pop into your gift box.

A Braided Raffia Lamp Mat

Materials Required: A bunch of raffia,

A bunch of coloured raffia,

A tapestry needle, No. 19.

Fig. 77

A lamp mat will be a welcome gift to mamma or even to your big brother for his room at college. The simplest one to make is of braided raffia. Take six pieces of raffia and tie them together at one end. Fasten this end to a nail or chair back, at a convenient height. If the raffia is dampened a little it will work more smoothly. Now braid it into a three-stranded plait, using two pieces for each strand. When a new piece is needed lay it above the end of the old one and continue. The ends are cut close after the braid is finished. You will need a great deal of this braided raffia—about ten yards of the natural colour and two or three of the coloured—but do a little at a time and you will find it pleasant work. When you have enough prepared, thread a No. 19 tapestry needle with a split strand of raffia and bind the end of it tightly around the end of the natural-coloured braid, taking a stitch or two through it to secure the binding. Now cut off the knot (which tied all six pieces together in starting) close to the binding and coil the braid into a tiny round centre. Run the needle through this centre back and forth, then start coiling the second row, bringing the long end of the braid around with its edge under the outer edge of the centre. The needle is run in slanting from right to left (see Fig. 77), then out from right to left, so that the stitches form a V within the coil. The whole mat is coiled and sewed in this way, except that when the last row of natural-coloured braid is stitched on, the end is bound as it was at the beginning and brought gradually in under the mat, where it is sewed securely. Be sure that you have finished a row before you end it off. This you can tell by counting the rows, from the centre out, on all sides of the mat. An end of the coloured braid (which is to form the border of the mat) is also bound with a split strand of coloured raffia and sewed against the under side of the mat. It is then sewed around like the rest of the mat, except that in the first row you will have to take great care to run the stitches through the natural-coloured braid so that they will not show. Be sure to finish the border at the part of the mat where it was started.

Sewed Raffia Lamp Mat

Materials Required: 12 or 14 yards of cotton clothesline or window cord,

A bunch of raffia,

A bunch of coloured raffia,

A No. 19 tapestry needle.

A soft, thick lamp mat that is beautiful to look at and very useful is quite simply made as follows:

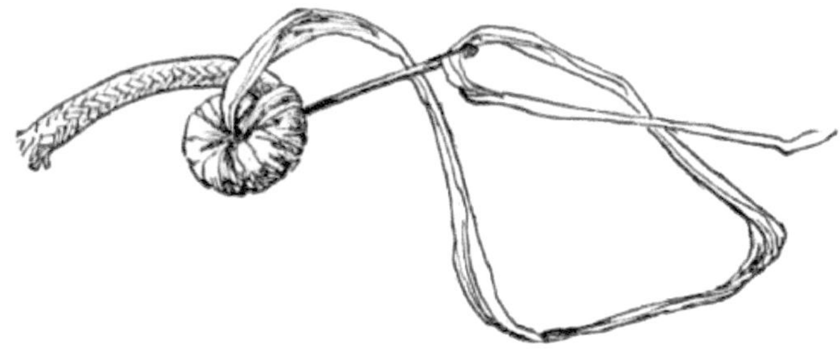

Fig. 78

Buy twelve or fourteen yards of cotton clothesline. It is white and smooth, and twisted like the fibre clothesline. Or there is a soft cotton window cord that is even better, because it is smoother. Thread a No. 19 tapestry needle with a strand of raffia, putting the thick, or root, end through the needle. Lay the other end of the raffia on the rope, with its tip turning toward the long end. Starting at the very end of the rope, wind the long end of raffia around it (and its own short end) for an inch or more. Then coil it into the smallest ring you possibly can, bring the long end of the raffia around, up through the centre of the ring and around again, taking in two coils—the one of which the ring was made and a second one made by bringing the long end of the rope around the ring (see Fig. 78). The first and second coils are covered in this way with a simple over-and-over stitch, which binds them together, passing around both and up through the centre. With the third coil the real stitch begins. It is an Indian one called the Figure Eight Stitch. The needle passes under the third coil (that is, the long end of rope which you are coiling around), around, over it, under the coil below, around, over it and up again, under and around the third coil—drawing the coils close together. The whole mat is sewed in this way. If you choose, you can work a design of coloured rings as a border or a solid border of the coloured raffia. Fig. 79 shows how the new pieces of raffia are added. Cross the old and new ends on the rope, bring the needle threaded with the new strand under the lower coil, out in front, over the lower coil, under and around the upper one, and so on.

Fig. 79

Doll's Hat of Raffia

Materials Required: A bunch of raffia,

A tapestry needle, No. 19.

How would you like to make a doll's raffia hat, as a birthday gift for one of your special friends—one that will fit her favourite doll? Of course it is to be a surprise, but you will have plenty of opportunities to measure the dolly's head. The raffia comes in so many colours that you will be able to choose one to match a special gown. When you are ready to begin, make five yards or more of braided raffia as described in the directions for the braided raffia lamp mat, and start the hat in the same way as the mat was begun, except that an oval instead of a round centre is formed. When you have made a large enough top for the crown, bring the coil of braid around, with its upper edge a little above the middle of the row just finished, drawing it quite tight, and in sewing make the stitches run like the twists in the braid—so that they will show as little as possible. The next row is sewed in the same way, and the next, until the crown is the height you wish. In starting the brim flatten the braid and bring it around more loosely. Be sure that each row of braid is sewed half way under the row to which you are stitching it. Make the whole brim in this way, keeping the braid always flat and loose so that it shall not pucker. When it is as large as you wish, you can make the edge roll slightly by drawing the last two rows quite tight as you sew them on. Fasten the end of the braid at the back of the hat by binding it with the raffia in your needle and stitching it firmly on the under side of the brim.

Leather Tag Case

Materials Required: A piece of heavy leather 3 ½ inches wide by 6 ½ inches long,

A piece of leather 3 ½ inches wide by 4 ½ inches long,

Some strips of leather ¼-inch wide,

Several kindergarten beads of a colour to match or harmonise with the leather,

A punch to make round holes,

2 dozen baggage tags,

Scissors,

A bodkin.

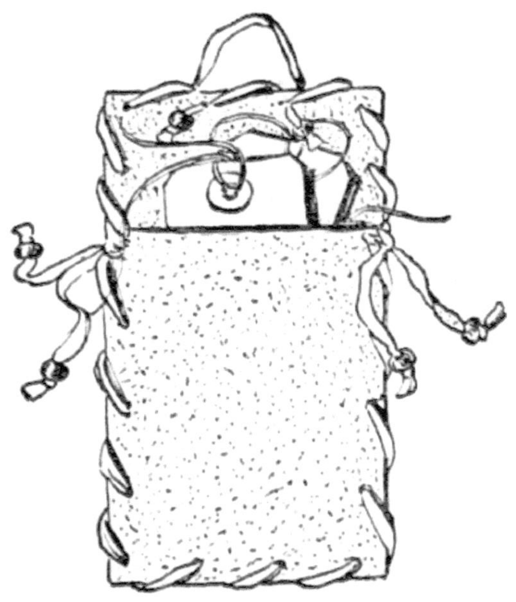

Leather Tag Case

One of the best presents a child can give to his father, or a man friend, is a leather case full of tags. Things made of leather are so handsome and durable that you cannot do better, in buying material for your gift box, than to invest in a skin of heavy leather in the natural colour, red or green. Another useful thing for your gift work will be a punch with which to make round holes in leather or cardboard. You will then only need a pair of scissors, a pencil and a few beads in order to be equipped not only to make this tag case but several other charming gifts. Measure and mark with pencil on the leather two pieces, one six inches and one-quarter long by three inches and one-half wide, the other four and one-half inches long by three and one-half inches wide, and cut them out carefully. Also cut a number of strips of leather a quarter of an inch wide and as long as the skin will allow. On each corner of the smaller piece of leather mark a dot three-sixteenths of an inch in from the edge. Then make three more dots the same distance from the edge and about an inch apart on each side, and two near the bottom, the same distance from the edge and each other. Now with your punch make holes through these dots. Lay this piece of leather on the larger one, with the lower edges and sides together, and with a pencil mark through the holes on the piece below. Dots are also made three-sixteenths of an inch in from the edge at each of the upper corners of the larger piece of leather, two about an inch apart at the middle of the top edge, and one more on either side, half way between the dots at the upper corners and the upper ones of those already marked from the smaller piece of leather. All these dots have holes punched through them. Now lay the pieces together, the smaller one on top, with its lower edge and sides fitting exactly with the bottom and sides of the larger piece. Starting at the upper right-hand corner of the smaller piece, bring a bodkin threaded with a long strip of leather up through the holes in both pieces, then up through the next hole below in both pieces, lacing them together all the way around to the other side. Here the bodkin is slipped off and the end is knotted with another strip of leather. On this new strip the bodkin is threaded and brought up through each hole in succession along the left side, the top and down the right side of the large piece of leather. It stops where the lacing began, and the ends are there tied together. A large bead is slipped on each of these ends and one on each of the two ends on the opposite side, and a knot is made at the tip to keep the bead from falling off. To make a loop to hang it by, thread the bodkin with a short strip of leather, run it down through the left of the two middle holes at the top of the case and out again through the right one. Cut it the length you wish the loop to be and thread a bead on each end, making a knot at the tip to keep the bead on.

Beaded Leather Pen Wiper

Materials Required: Two circular pieces of leather about 3 ½ inches in diameter,

3 circular pieces of natural-coloured chamois about

3 inches in diameter,

A strip of leather ¼-inch wide and ¼ yard long,

1 skein of beads, No. 3-0,

1 skein of beads, No. 3-0, of another colour.

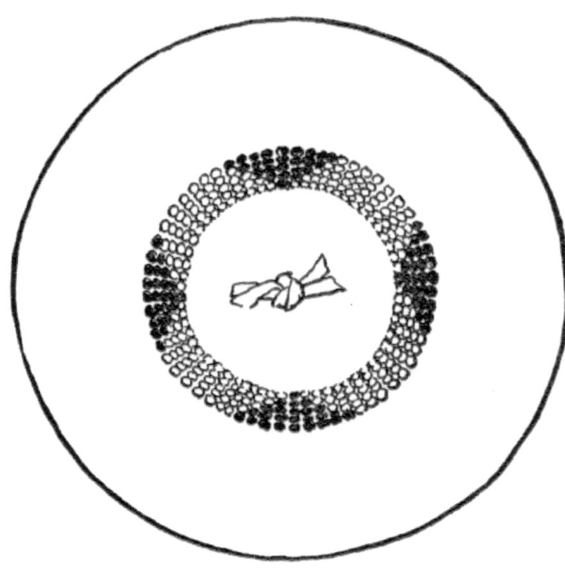

Fig. 80

A pen wiper is such a usual present that you may think no one would care for it, but look around and you will surely find a big brother or sister, or perhaps a friend, who hasn't one. And this is such an interesting pen wiper to make. It is very simple, just two round pieces of leather and three of chamois. The top piece of leather has the design shown in Fig. 80 worked on it in beads of a colour that will look well with the leather you have chosen. Black and crystal beads will harmonise with red leather or dark-green crystal and opaque white. If the leather is not so bright a colour, the beads may be more gay. Work the design with the stitch described in the directions for making an Indian beaded shirt in Chapter V., bringing the strings of beads farther apart at the outer edge of the circle than on the inside. When the beadwork is done, put the pieces of leather together with the chamois ones between, mark two dots a quarter of an inch apart at the centre of the top, punch holes through the dots and then through the other pieces of chamois and leather. A bodkin threaded with a strip of leather is then run down through one hole, up through the other, and the ends are knotted together and cut quite short.

Baby's Worsted Ball

Materials Required: A piece of thin cardboard a foot square,

Odds and ends of worsted,

A worsted needle,

A piece of string,

Scissors.

We have not made any plans, as yet, for a gift for the baby. Suppose we make him a great, fluffy worsted ball. Among your mother's odds and ends of worsted you will find plenty of gay colours that will be exactly what you want. Then you will need some thin cardboard, or bristol board. On this mark two circles, five inches in diameter, and at the centre of each of these, two smaller circles an inch and a quarter in diameter. Cut out the two large circles and the small holes within them. You will then have two circular pieces of cardboard with a round hole in the centre of each, making it look like a cookie. Take a strong but slender piece of string about a foot long and lay it around the hole in the centre of one of the pieces of cardboard, with the ends coming together below the outer edge (see Fig. 81). Lay the other piece of cardboard directly over the first one and hold them firmly together (see Fig. 82) while with a needle threaded with worsted you sew around and around the cardboard rings, bringing the needle each time through the hole in the centre and around the outer edge of both rings. When a needleful of worsted is finished leave the end hanging and start another. Keep on until the hole in the middle is quite filled up and the whole thing looks like a puffy cushion. Now take a sharp pair of scissors and cut the layers of worsted at the outer edge of the paste-board rings all the way around. Do this carefully but quickly, and be sure not to cut the two ends of string, for now is the time to use them. They are tied together just as tightly as possible, and as close to the centre. The cardboard rings are then slipped out, leaving a soft, fluffy ball of many colours. Clip off the uneven ends of worsted here and there, and the ball will be complete.

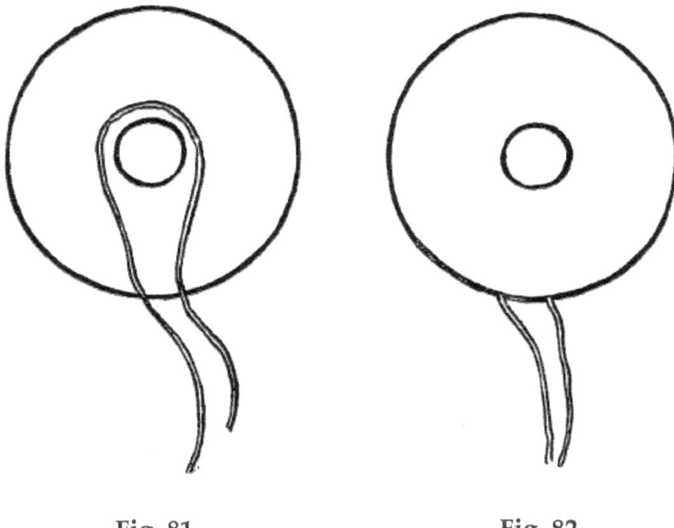

Fig. 81   **Fig. 82**

Raffia sewed in the same way over tiny cardboard rings, then tied and cut, makes fascinating little pompons for a doll's hat.

CHAPTER IX
PAPER FLOWERS AND TOYS

Fig. 83

It sometimes seems, on a rainy day, as if there was nothing to do because you have not the materials that are needed for certain occupations—but there is always paper. You may not, of course, have all the things that are used in making tissue-paper flowers, unless you have been so thrifty as to buy them, looking forward to just such a time as this. But if you cannot make the flowers at once, you can decide which ones you wish to do and plan a list of the materials you will need. Then there are numbers of things that you can fashion from watercolour paper, or even heavy note paper and cardboard; so let us get out pencil and paper, paste and scissors, and begin.

Materials Required: 2 large sheets of linen writing paper

1 sheet of deep-yellow tissue paper,

1 sheet of olive-green tissue paper,

A little cotton batting,

A long wire stem,

A tube of paste,

Pen and ink,

Scissors.

Fig. 84

How would you like to make a game of your very own with which you and your brothers and sisters or some of your friends can play? It is quite simple—just a great paper daisy with a slip of paper pasted on the under side of each petal. Upon each slip is written a sort of conundrum, the answer to which is the name of a plant or flower. If you can get a real daisy for a model, so much the better.

Fold a large sheet of linen writing paper diagonally so that you will have a square eight by eight inches. Bend it over again diagonally, and then again and again, so that it will have been folded four times in all. Now draw the outline of a daisy petal upon the folded paper (see Fig. 83), and cut it out through all the thicknesses. This will give you a sixteen-petaled daisy. The centre has next to be made. Cut from deep-yellow tissue paper eight circles three inches across, six circles two inches, and six an inch across. This is easily done by folding the paper into as many thicknesses as you wish circles of each size, so that you can cut through them all at once. Before separating the circles cut the edges into a fine fringe about three-eighths of an inch deep. Fold a piece of olive-green tissue paper in the same way as the white paper for the petals was folded, but once more, and cut it like Fig. 84. This is for the calyx. Next cut some slips of paper just large enough to be pasted on the underside of the petals and write on each a number and a conundrum from the following list:

1. A public building in Philadelphia.

2. A plant that rhymes with pansy.

3. A foolish wild animal.

4. A wise man.

5. Fit for a king.

6. A girl's name.

7. A plant for Sundays.

8. For thirsty folk.

9. Several droves of sheep.

10. Part of a pet.

11. Two girls' names.

12. Something that we know flies, though no one has ever seen it.

13. A rosy athlete.

14. A necessary article of food and a piece of china.

15. A girl's name and a metal.

16. An animal and a covering for the hand.

The following key, or answers to the conundrums, you will of course keep hidden until after the game has been played:

1. Mint

2. Tay

3. Dandelion.

4. Sage.

5. Goldenrod.

6. Sumach (Sue Mack).

7. Jack-in-the-pulpit.

8. Pitcher-plant.

9. Phlox (Flocks).

10. Cattail.

11. Rosemary.

12. Thyme.

13. Scarlet runner.

14. Buttercup.

15. Marigold.

16. Foxglove.

When the slips have each been pasted on a petal the daisy is put together in this way: Take a long, stout piece of wire, such as is sold for paper-flower stems; put the yellow circles all together, the larger ones at the bottom, then the medium ones and the smallest on top. Bend one end of the wire into a tiny ring and run the other end down through the centre of the yellow circles, then through the middle of the white circle with the petals on its edge, putting a touch of paste between the centre and the petals. Now paste a thin layer of cotton batting to the lower side of the petal-edged piece, at the centre, and run the wire stem through the middle of the green calyx, pasting the paper lightly to the cotton. Wind the stem with olive-green tissue paper cut in strips two inches wide, and cut from the same paper some leaves as much as possible like the little leaves of a daisy plant. The directions for playing this game are given in chapter X.

How to Make a Country Girl

Materials Required: A sheet of brown paper,

A sheet of heavy watercolour paper, 6 by 8 inches,

A pencil,

A box of watercolour paints,

Scissors.

Fig. 85

Little country girls are almost always useful, and though this one is only made of paper she can be useful too. She will serve as a dinner card or a penwiper, or even carry courtplaster to those who need it. If you do not care for any of these things you can play with her, for she makes a charming paper doll. Fig. 85 shows one side of the little girl, the other is just the same. She is made as follows: Cut from brown paper the pattern shown in Fig. 86, making it six and a half inches high by four and three-eighths inches broad—at the widest point. Take care to mark the dotted lines exactly where they are in the picture. It will be better to draw the apron, sunbonnet and little shoes on the pattern, for then you can copy directly from it instead of from the smaller one in the book. Lay the pattern on a piece of heavy watercolour paper and draw around it with a sharp-pointed pencil, marking the dotted lines exactly. Next the little girl must be cut out. Do this carefully with a pair of small, sharp scissors. Bend the paper on the dotted lines so that it will look like Fig. 85. On all the lines except the one down the front A (see Fig. 86) and the two marked B the paper is bent forward, on these two it turns back and the flaps on the bottom of the shoes are turned back. Now for the finishing touches. For these you will need pen and ink and a box of watercolour paints. The dress, where it peeps out beyond the white apron, the bands on the sleeves and the dots and edge of the sunbonnet, should all be painted some pretty colour—pink, red, blue, green or yellow—whatever you choose. The shoes should be black, and the outlines of the apron and pockets, the gathers of the sleeves and sunbonnet are all drawn in black ink.

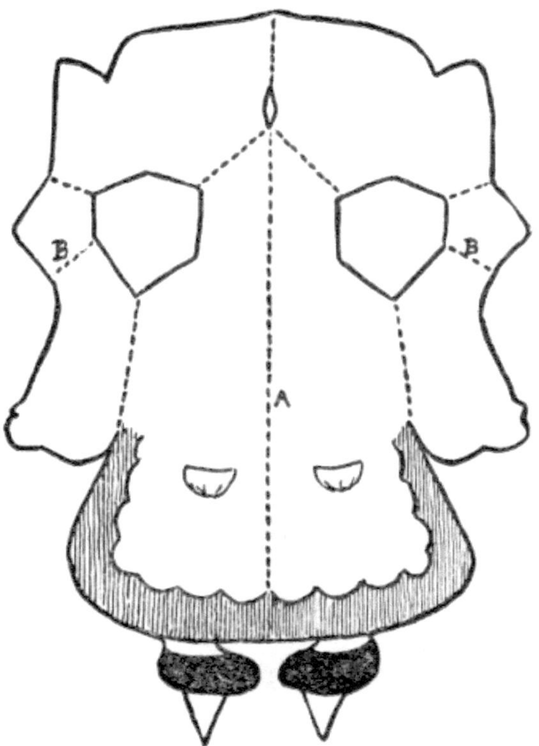

Fig. 86

Fig. 87

The little girl is now complete unless you wish to have her stand by herself, in which case cut a circular piece of cardboard and glue her upon it by the flaps on her shoes. If you would like to make her useful, you can attach two or three tiny sheets of courtplaster between her skirts or several leaves of flannel, so that she can serve as a penwiper.

Fig. 88

A Paper Santa Claus

Materials Required: The same as for the Country Girl.

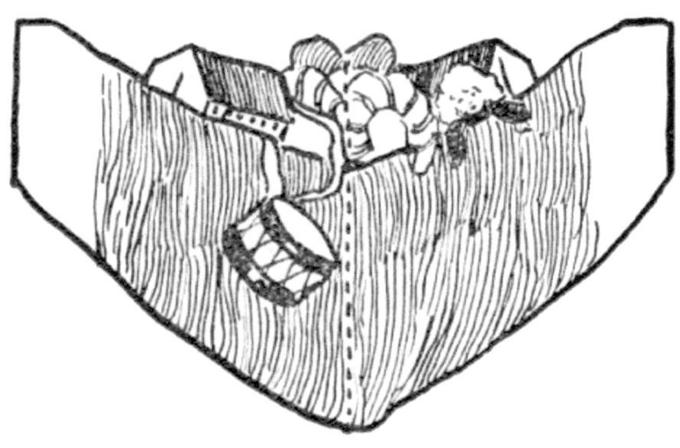

Fig. 89

Another delightful little paper person made on the plan of the Country Girl is the Santa Claus shown in Fig. 87. He makes a charming Christmas card to carry greetings or a gift. The pattern (see Fig. 88) is made five and one-eighth inches high by five and a quarter inches wide, of brown paper, in the same way as the pattern of the country girl. Santa Claus is also cut from watercolour paper and bent according to the dotted lines. The colouring should be red and white, of course, with a green holly wreath. It would not do to forget the Saint's pack, which is cut from the pattern shown in Fig. 89. It is painted brown, with gaily coloured toys—dolls, drums and Noah's arks—peeping out at the top. Paste it between the two sides of Santa Claus near his shoulders.

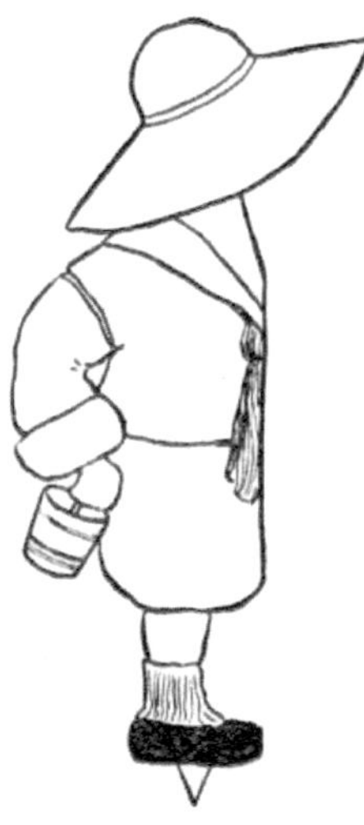

Fig. 90

A Seashore Boy

Materials Required: The same as for the Country Girl.

As a companion for the Country Girl you can make, if you like, a Seashore Boy (see Fig. 90) in just the same way. The pattern given in Fig. 91 shows where the paper is to be folded. From all the folds the paper should bend backward except on the lines marked A, from these it bends forward. The colouring should be mostly blue and white. The great sun hat will be straw coloured, of course, with a blue band. His short socks are of white, with brown legs showing above them, and his suit should be blue, or a white one with a blue tie. The pail may be painted red.

A Valentine Favour

Materials Required: A piece of watercolour paper a foot square,

A box of watercolour paints,

A strip of scarlet china silk 5 inches wide by ½ yard long,

A yard of scarlet baby ribbon,

A spool of scarlet sewing silk,

A bodkin,

A tube of paste,

Scissors.

Fig. 91

A boy or girl with deft fingers can make the most attractive little valentine favour imaginable in a short time and at very slight expense. It is a double heart of watercolour paper, painted scarlet and with a silk puff of the same colour drawn up at the top, making a bag for bonbons.

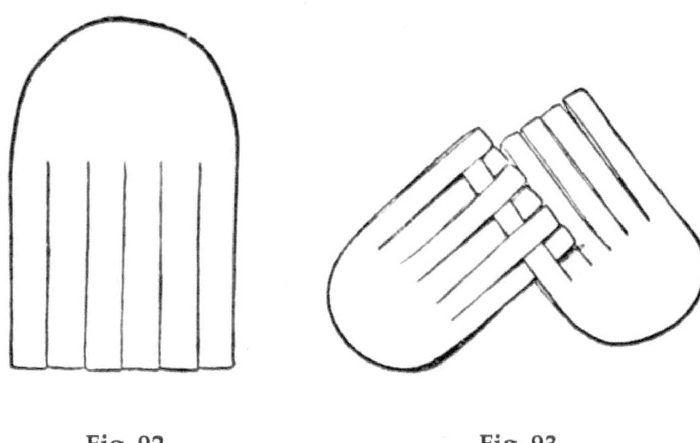

Fig. 92   Fig. 93

The heart is perhaps the most difficult part, but a child who has learned in kindergarten to weave with paper will be able to do it without much trouble. Cut from watercolour paper two pieces in the shape shown in Fig. 92. The paper should be doubled and the fold laid against the straight edge at the bottom of the pattern. The size does not matter very much, though if the heart is to hold anything the pieces should measure four inches and a quarter from the doubled edge to the top of the rounded end and two and five-eighths inches across. Rule with pencil a light line across each piece at two and five-eighths inches from the straight end. Five lines are also ruled in the other direction, the first one seven-sixteenths of an inch from one side of each piece of paper and the others the same distance apart (see Fig. 92). Cut along these lines with sharp, strong scissors from the double straight edge to the ruled line near the top of each piece. The lower part of both pieces will thus be cut into doubled strips. Now take a piece in each hand, rounded end down, and weave the lower strip of the piece in your right hand through the strips in the left-hand piece. As the strips are double, the weaving must be done rather differently than with single strips of paper. The strip with which you are weaving goes around the first strip in the left-hand piece, through the next one, around the next, and so on (see Fig. 93). When it comes to the end it is pushed down a little way and the next strip on the right is woven above it, only that this one passes through the strips that the first one passed around, and around those that the first one passed through. Weave one after another until all six of the strips in the right-hand piece are woven in with those on the left—when it should open to form a heart-shaped bag, as shown in Fig. 94.

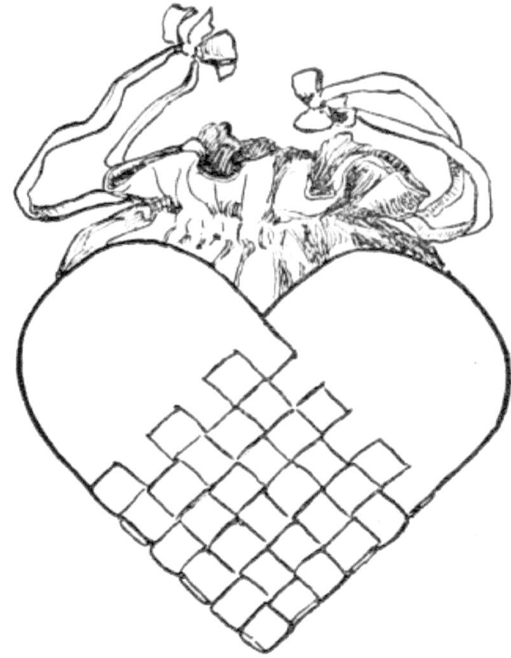

Fig. 94

Colour the heart on both sides with vermilion watercolour paint and it will then be ready for the silk top. Cut from scarlet China silk a strip five inches wide by half a yard long. Sew the ends together, hem the top and make a casing for the ribbon drawstring, as described in the directions for the beaded silk bag in chapter V. The lower edge is gathered to fit the inside of the top of the heart and pasted into it on a straight line, running just below the openings, around both sides of the heart. If the paste is not very sticky you may need to take a tiny stitch here and there with scarlet sewing silk, tacking the silk top more securely to the heart. It will then be ready to line with a lace paper doily or some waxed paper, and fill with bonbons.

A Frog Jumping Jack

Materials Required: A small sheet of 4-ply bristol board,

A box of watercolour paints,

A ball of fine white string,

Pen and ink,

A pair of sharp scissors,

A large, sharp-pointed worsted needle.

Fig. 95

There is a funny frog jumping jack that you can make if you like some cheer-less, rainy day. He brings smiles wherever he goes.

Fig. 96

Take a sheet of heavy four-ply bristol board and draw upon it the pieces shown in Figs. 95, 96, 97 and 98—the frog's head and body, legs and one arm. Make them as large as you can. The head and body together should measure eight inches high by seven wide, from the right side to the end of the mandolin on the left. The legs should be about six and a half inches long and the right arm should of course be the size of the left, which is drawn on the same piece as the body. Colour the body, throat and legs pale yellow with watercolour paint; the upper part of the head, the arms and the outer edges of the body and legs are first painted light green and then marked with irregular spots and dashes of medium and dark bluish green. A red ribbon with a Maltese cross of the same colour is painted around his neck, and the mandolin he holds is white above and black underneath. The eyes should be dark green with very large whites, and the smiling mouth red, of course. The strings of the mandolin are drawn with pen and ink, as are the outlines of the whites of the eyes, the hands and feet. Now Mr. Frog must be put together. Tie a knot in a piece of fine white string and thread the other end through a large worsted needle. Run the needle through the frog's body at the lower right side (where you see the dot on Fig. 95), leaving the knot in front, pass it through the right leg about half an inch from the top and fasten it with a knot at the back. The other leg is attached in the same way, and the right arm is placed in position and fastened to the body as the legs were. A knot is then made in a piece of white cord and the end is brought through the right arm (leaving the knot in front) about three-quarters of an inch below where it is fastened to the body, and near the outer edge of the arm. The end of the string is brought down at the back of the frog, quite loosely, to the upper part of the right leg, where it passes through and is tied to the part of the string that comes from the arm (see Fig. 99). It is then brought across to the top of the left leg, where it is tied. A separate string fifteen inches long is attached to the centre of the piece, which passes from one leg to the other (this is the one that is pulled to make him jump), and a short loop of string is fastened at the top of his head by which to hold him. When the long string is pulled Mr. Frog will dance and play the mandolin.

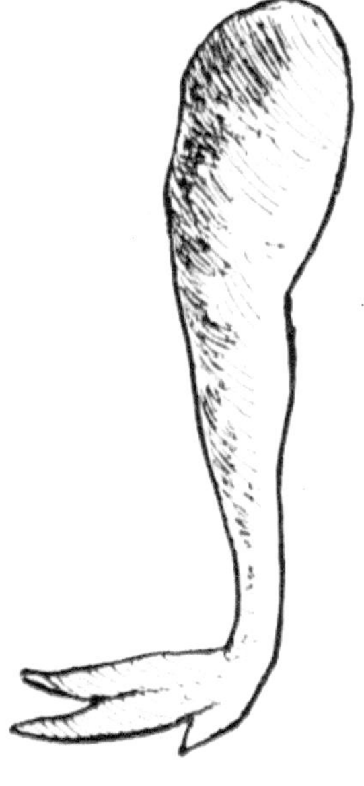

Fig. 97

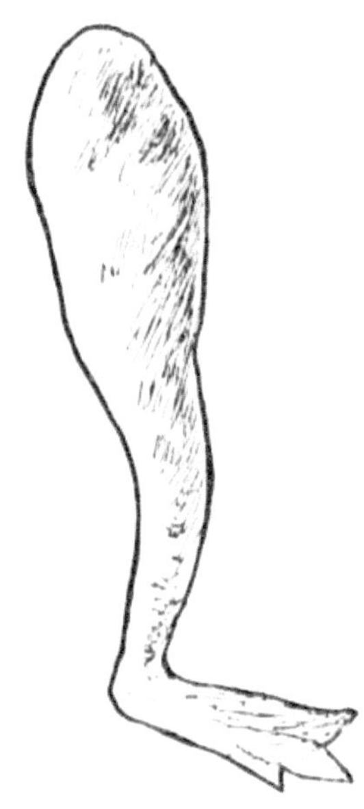

Fig. 98

Paper Flowers

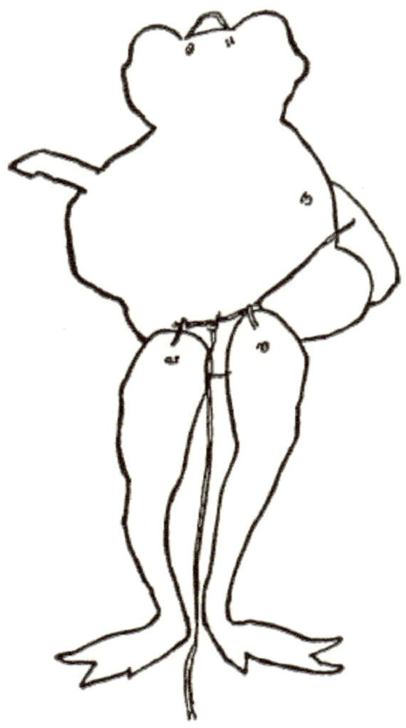

Fig. 99

Have you ever made paper flowers? If not, you have probably seen them made by the cardboard patterns which dealers in tissue paper sell. How about making the patterns yourself—for the poppies, daisies and tulips and all the other flowers. It will be an interesting thing to do and not difficult. Catch one of the poppy petals as it floats off from the flower, blown by a summer breeze. Notice that there are only four petals (if it is a single poppy), the two smaller ones setting across the larger pair below. Poppies are charming and much simpler than other flowers to copy in paper. You may have noticed that the petals of the real ones look almost exactly like silky, crinkled paper. Draw an outline of the petal a little larger than life on heavy brown paper. Fold the paper back at the base of the petal and cut it out in the two thicknesses so that it will look like Fig. 100. The two lower petals will be cut in the same way but larger. You now have a pattern for as many poppies as you choose. They can be made in various colours—white, red, pink, pink and white and yellow. You can buy poppy centres ready to use, or if you prefer you can make them yourself in this way: For a poppy four and a half inches across, cut a circle of yellow paper an inch and a quarter in diameter. Fringe the edge about half an inch. Next take a wire stem, bend the end into a small circle, cover it with a tiny ball of cotton batting and over this a piece of olive-green tissue paper, forming it to look as much as possible like the real poppy centre (see Fig. 101). Wind the edges of the paper close around the wire stem. Now run the other end of the stem down through the yellow circle, brushing it with paste to attach it to the green part of the centre. Slip the smaller pair of petals on the stem, then the larger pair (with a little paste between), so that the smaller pair will set directly across the larger. This completes the poppy. The stem is wound with strips of olive-green tissue paper, and the leaves are cut from the same paper by a pattern which you can easily make by laying a poppy leaf on a sheet of cardboard and drawing around it with a sharp-pointed pencil.

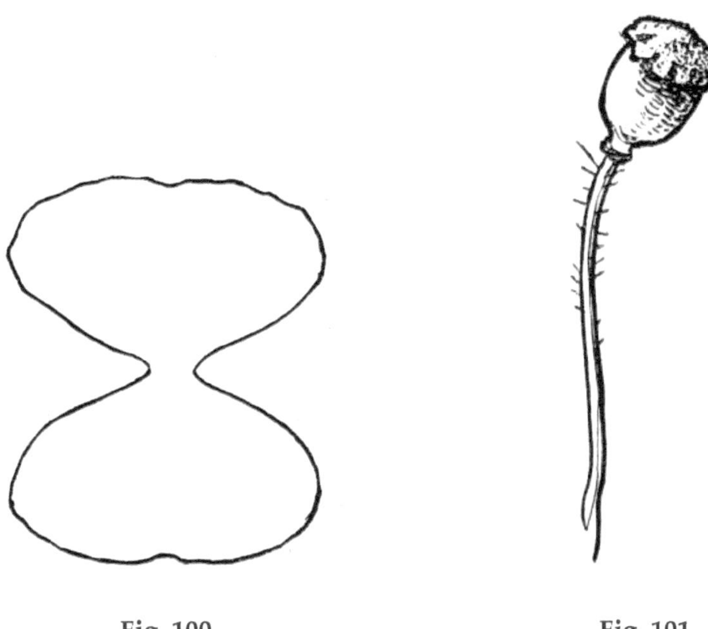

Fig. 100   Fig. 101

Ox-Eyed Daisies

Materials Required: 1 or more sheets of deep-yellow tissue paper,

A sheet of olive-green tissue paper,

A ball of dark-brown worsted,

Several wire stems,

A tube of paste,

Scissors.

Ox-eyed daisies are easily fashioned and look so like the real ones that they are as satisfactory as any paper flowers you can make. Take four thicknesses of deep-yellow tissue paper. Bend the corner over diagonally and cut a square four by four inches. Next fold the paper in the same way as for the petals described in the Daisy Game in this chapter. Mark on the top of the last fold a petal, as shown in Fig. 83, and cut it out through all the thicknesses. After it is unfolded you may have to cut some of the petals up nearer to the centre. Wind some brown worsted around your thumb about twenty times, take it off and run through it the end of a wire stem which has been bent into a tiny crook. Tie the worsted centre just above the wire with a short piece of worsted, or bind it with fine wire, and cut the loops at the top. Now run the other end of the stem down through the centre of the petals. Make a green calyx like the one for the white daisy but much smaller, not over an inch across. Wind the stem with strips of olive-green tissue paper, laying in every now and then a daisy leaf cut from the same dark-green paper. Other single flowers can be as easily made as this, and you will find that the patterns will not be difficult to make if you take the natural flowers for your models.

A Curled Chrysanthemum

Materials Required: Several sheets of pink or yellow tissue paper in a light and medium shade,

Several sheets of olive-green tissue paper,

A small piece of cardboard,

Some wire stems,

A tube of paste,

Scissors.

Fig. 102

Chrysanthemums are among the most natural of paper flowers, and fascinating to make. White ones are pretty, and those that are made of shades of pink or yellow are even more attractive. Cut the pattern shown in Fig. 102 from cardboard and lay it on three thicknesses of medium yellow tissue paper, seven and a half inches square, which have been folded diagonally three times. Hold the pattern firmly upon it and cut it out carefully. Then in the same way cut two thicknesses of light-yellow paper into petals. A piece of olive-green tissue paper is folded into a smaller square and cut in the same way, to make a calyx. To curl the petals, put a small sofa cushion on your knee, lay a petal upon it, and, taking a common hatpin with a smooth, round head, press it upon the end of each petal up to the centre. This will curl it as if by magic. Do another and another till the whole piece is finished. Then curl a second piece and a third in the same way. When they are all done bend a long wire stem at one end and run the other end through the centre of the petal-edged pieces, which should be laid one above the other, the darker ones on top. Put a touch of paste between them, slip on the green calyx, wind the stem with strips of green tissue paper, laying in a chrysanthemum leaf from time to time, and the flower is complete.

Making a Chrysanthemum

CHAPTER X
GAMES FOR TWO OR THREE TO PLAY

On stormy days the children of a family are likely to be alone—unless they are so fortunate as to have a little visitor in the house, or a friend who lives near wraps up and comes to play with them. A child who is alone can read, or find in the other chapters of this book some absorbing occupation; for a party of children there are always plenty of games, but it is sometimes difficult to think of a game that two or three will enjoy. The following are a few suggestions for such an emergency:

Picture Puzzles

Materials Required: As many pieces of cardboard about 6 by 8 inches as there are children,

As many pairs of scissors as there are children,

One or more tubes of paste,

Several old magazines.

There is such a fascination about cutting and pasting that a game like this is one of the best you can choose for a dull day. Each child has an old magazine, a piece of cardboard and a pair of scissors, while tubes of paste lie conveniently near. When the children are seated around a table the game begins. It is played in this way: Each player cuts from his magazine a picture (which must be smaller than his card), pastes it upon his piece of cardboard, and when it is dry and firm cuts it in pieces with six straight cuts of the scissors, so as to make a puzzle. He then mixes the pieces and passes them to his neighbour on the right. At a given signal each child tries to put the puzzle which he has received together as quickly as possible. The one who finishes first calls out that he is through, and he is of course the winner.

As a sequel the children will enjoy colouring the puzzles. If they are pretty and neatly made they may be given to a child's hospital, to amuse some other little children in the long days of convalescence.

How to Play the Daisy Game

This is a good guessing game for two or more children to play, and if you will follow the directions given in chapter IX. you will find that it can be made quite easily. None of the players should have seen the key, or answers to the conundrum, but if you find that they have seen it, you can write on the slips of paper, instead of the conundrums, the names of flowers with the letters mixed for example, sapyn, for pansy. Each child in turn pulls a petal from the daisy and tries to guess the name of the flower, which is the answer to the conundrum written on the under side of the petal. Five minutes is the time allowed, and if the player has not guessed the flower in that time he must pass the petal to the child on his left, who also has five minutes in which to guess it. If he guesses correctly the petal belongs to him, and at the end of the game the player having the most petals has won.

Horses in the Stable

Materials Required: A pasteboard shoe box,

Some marbles,

Pen and ink,

Scissors.

Although this game is played with marbles, girls as well as boys will enjoy it, and it is so easily prepared that it can be played at short notice. Take a long pasteboard box—a shoe box is about the right size. Remove the cover and turn it upside down. Now, starting at the lower edge, draw five doorways, like those shown in Fig. 103. The one in the centre should be an inch across and an inch and a half high, the two on each side of it an inch and a half wide and two inches high, and the outer ones each two inches wide and two and a half inches high. Cut out these doorways with a sharp, strong pair of scissors and mark over the middle one in pen and ink the number 25. The two on either side of it have marked above them 10, and the other two each have 5. Stand the box, or stable, thus prepared, against the wall and place a mark four feet from it. Each player has three marbles, and in turn tries to roll or shoot them from the mark through the little doors into the box. If he succeeds in putting one through the smallest door he makes twenty-five; if through either of the other doors his score is increased by the number marked above it. There should be a time limit for the game—half an hour, for example. The score of each player, which is kept on a sheet of paper, is added at the end of that time and the one having the most points has won the game.

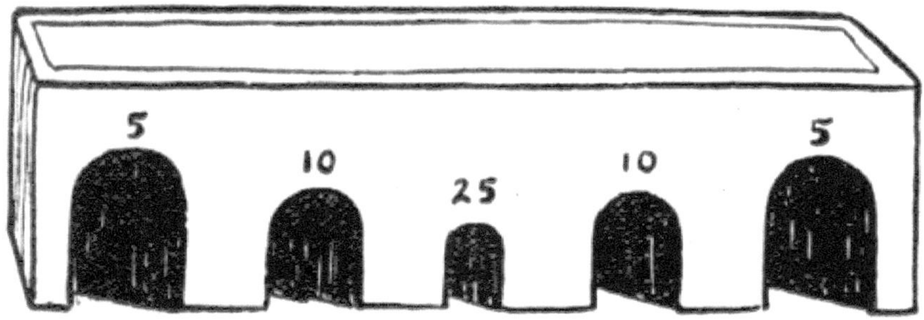

Fig. 103

Plants and Flowers

Materials Required: As many pencils and sheets of paper as players,

A large sheet of cardboard,

Some seed catalogues,

A tube of paste,

Scissors.

Although a number of children can play this game, two or three will enjoy it quite as well. Any boy or girl can make it. You will need first of all a number of seed catalogues. Cut from these eighteen or twenty pictures of flowers and plants, taking care not to leave the names on them. Write in pencil, on the back of each, a number (any one from 1 to 18) and the name—this is for your own guidance later on. Now make a list of the flowers and plants, each with its number before it. This is the key, to be put away till after the game is played. Take a large sheet of cardboard, about twenty by twenty-four inches, and paste upon it the flowers and plants in the order of their numbers, marking the number of each clearly in pen and ink underneath it. If you like you can colour the pictures—this will make the game more attractive, of course, and as you can use it many times it is worth while. A loop of string, by which to hang it, should be run through the top of the card at the centre. When you are ready to play the game hang the cardboard sheet where all can see it; give each player a pencil and a piece of paper, on the left side of which numbers from 1 to 18 have been marked. Each child tries in the time allowed—about twenty minutes—to guess the names of the flowers and plants on the sheet or cardboard, and write each opposite its number on his piece of paper. The correct names are then read from the key and the players check off their guesses. The one who has guessed the greatest number correctly is of course the winner.

A Ball-and-Fan Race

Materials Required: 2 Japanese paper balls,

2 palmleaf fans.

Two children will find this race an interesting one for a rainy day. The best place in which to play it is a large room with very little furniture in it—a playroom for example. Each player stands at a corner of the room diagonally opposite the other, three feet out from the corner, and each has a Japanese paper ball in front of him and a large fan in his hand. They must face different ways and both count together "One, two, three, and away!" As they finish counting, the children begin to fan their balls around the room, close to the wall. There will be some lively skirmishing when they meet, as they are likely to do when half way around the room. Then each tries to send his opponent's ball back and his own forward. When each finally gets his ball back to the corner where he started, he must try to send it as quickly as possible to the middle of the room, where a chair is placed. The ball must be fanned through the legs of this chair and to the goal of his opponent. The player who first accomplishes this is the winner.

A Ball-and-Fan Race

Fun with Popcorn

Materials Required: An open fire,

A corn popper,

Several ears of popcorn,

A prize, if desired.

If the open fire burns brightly in your playroom, no matter how gray and bleak the day may be outside, you and your brothers and sisters can keep warm and cheerful over this delightful game. You may provide a prize for the winner, if you like, but the only things that are absolutely necessary are the fire, some popcorn and a popper. When the players are seated in a semicircle around the fire they may all help in shelling the corn. After this is done, divide the popcorn evenly between them, so that each shall have a small quantity. The player on the left side of the fireplace now takes the corn popper and pops his corn. When it is done, the kernels that are fully popped are counted, also the unpopped ones, and a record is made of each. The next player pops his corn and counts the result, and so on until all have finished. The child having the largest number of fully popped kernels is the winner, and may receive a prize. Afterward the winner and the defeated players will equally enjoy eating the fluffy popcorn, or if the cook is particularly amiable they may be allowed to flock to the kitchen and make popcorn balls.

Express

Materials Required: 12 or 15 articles, large and small, light and heavy.

This is a lively game that needs little preparation. All you will have to provide is a number of articles, toys, pieces of china (not valuable ones), a glass of water, some very small things and one or more large ones, something heavy like a dumb-bell or flatiron and something light—a palmleaf fan, for example. When you have them all collected, on a table or stand on one side of the room where the game is to be played, place another table or stand across the room. Then you must have a clock or a watch, and that is all—except the players. Each child in turn takes one thing at a time, from the stand where the various articles are piled, and carries it to the table at the opposite side of the room. It is done as quickly as possible, for the object is to move everything from one place to the other in the least possible time. Each player is timed and his record kept on a piece of paper. If a player drops any-thing he must carry it back to the starting point and make another trip with it. The next player begins at the table to which the first one took the baggage and carries it, in the same way, back to the first table. So it goes on until everyone has played expressman. The player who succeeds in transferring the baggage in the shortest time is, of course, the winner.

A Hurdle Race

Materials Required: A box of tiddledywinks,

A sheet of white cardboard,

A box of watercolour paints,

A pencil,

Scissors,

A ball of white string,

Some pins.

The next time you are kept indoors by the weather, you and a brother or sister may enjoy a hurdle race. It is played with tiddledywink chips and pasteboard hurdles on a large table or on the floor. You can make the hurdles yourself. They should be cut from cardboard, eight inches wide and four inches high. Paint some of them with wooden bars and others green—like high hedges. In making the hurdles, cut the cardboard so that a strip two inches deep by an inch across will extend below each lower corner (see Fig. 104). One of these is bent sharply forward at the place marked by the dotted lines, the other is turned back, forming stands to keep the hurdles upright.

The racecourse will have to be laid out on a covered table or carpeted floor, as the tiddledywinks can only be used on a soft, cushiony surface. You can make the boundaries with white string, held in place here and there with pins. An oval course, though more difficult to mark is rather more exciting than a straight one, but either will do. Have the course eight inches wide and as long as you please. The hurdles may be placed where-ever you choose, but be sure to have plenty of them.

Fig. 104

When you are ready to begin, each player takes a large tiddledywink chip and a small one of the same colour—but different from his opponent's—and at a signal given by a third person, who acts as umpire, the race begins. Snap the tiddledy-wink chip just as you do in playing the game, only taking great care not to send it out of the course, for if it goes outside the lines you must set it back three inches. The umpire follows the race, of course, and settles all disputed questions.

Pictures from Fairy Tales

Materials Required: A number of old magazines,

Twice as many sheets of cardboard or heavy brown paper, 10 by 12 inches, as there are children,

As many pairs of scissors as there are children,

A tube of paste for each child.

Two or three children who know and love the old fairy tales can spend a delightful hour playing this game. Each one should have several old magazines and a sheet of cardboard, as well as scissors and a tube of paste. The leader, who may be one of the children or an older person, explains the game as follows: Each child is expected to make a picture on his sheet of cardboard to illustrate some fairy tale. It is not necessary to draw it; he can cut from the magazines people and properties and scenery and paste them upon the card. He must be sure not to tell anyone the story he has chosen. At the end of half an hour the pictures should be finished. A bell is rung for everyone to stop work and the pictures are placed where all can see them. The leader now holds one up before the children and asks them what story they suppose it illustrates, and what particular part of the story. The child who answers first wins the picture. The other pictures are held up, one at a time, and the children try to see who can guess them first. If they are ready for another round of the game after this one is finished, they may find it amusing to vary it by making pictures from "Mother Goose."

Lector House believes that a society develops through a two-fold approach of continuous learning and adaptation, which is derived from the study of classic literary works spread across the historic timeline of literature records. Therefore, we aim at reviving, repairing and redeveloping all those inaccessible or damaged but historically as well as culturally important literature across subjects so that the future generations may have an opportunity to study and learn from past works to embark upon a journey of creating a better future.

This book is a result of an effort made by Lector House towards making a contribution to the preservation and repair of original ancient works which might hold historical significance to the approach of continuous learning across subjects.

HAPPY READING & LEARNING!

LECTOR HOUSE LLP
E-MAIL: lectorpublishing@gmail.com